Exodus
from
darkness
to
light

by

Rita Albadran
English Translation

Rita Albadran's contact address and email:

P. O. Box 1143,   Upland, CA 91786

galbadran@hotmail.com

Cover image: Philipp K.

Contents

Introduction

I will give thanks to the LORD with all my heart. I will declare all your wonderful deeds (Psalm 9:1).

The work that God does in the human heart is a real miracle, and when it happens, the person is eager to tell about it. According to the words of the Lord:

Go home to your people and tell them what great things the Lord has done for you and how he had mercy on you (Mark 5:19).

Imagine how much the salvation of Muslims means to me. I consider it a huge miracle without measure. And in spite of threats of death by the Islamic sword for anyone who wants to clarify the truth about the Islamic darkness, we will continue to see God's miraculous intervention to turn them from death to life.

And we can see great strength in the Muslims who accept Jesus, in the way they tell their salvation story, and how God fills the

i

emptiness that they suffer, and how God opens their eyes to see the real light, and to become children of the Lord, heirs of the Holy Kingdom of endless glory, which transcends the physical realm and the lusts of the flesh.

This book is about the exodus of "Rita," the story of the miracle that happened in her life, the witness to the work of Christ in helping her to cross from the darkness to the light and from Islamic slavery to the freedom of the sons and daughters of God.

I pray God will use this book to save the souls of those who read it. Amen.

Father Zakaria Botros

Al-Fady Sat. Channel

Preface

My Gratitude to my Lord is unique, different from any other person's gratitude.

I am a woman who comes from Iraq, my family's homeland, a land of security and war, a land of joy and pain. I am a runaway. A runaway from Islam, from persecution, from chains, and heartbreak. I was a stranger in many strange lands. I tasted much of loneliness, betrayal, hunger, and cold. And, oh, how often I walked in foreign countries, weeping tears of grief and pain!

I was born into a religion that I was taught to think of as grand and glorious—a giant full of strength and philosophical wisdom. But I was living shackled to the chains of Islam without being allowed to try to make sense of any of it.

If I asked a question about one of the verses (ayat) of the Quran, I was told, "It is forbidden!"

If I wanted to know the truth about Muhammad, "It is forbidden!"

I wasn't just born a Muslim. Islam was like a stamp that was branded not only on my passport and my name, but also my flesh. There was no escape to the outside.

But, as for my heart, no one on earth could touch it. They could control my external life, but not what was inside me.

I was a prisoner until my Lord came and, in love, touched my heart and freed me with His blood. I testify here that His name is Jesus. He stretched His hand and wrenched me by the roots. There was much pain in that wrench. I wept until I almost drowned in my tears. But He had a grand purpose for plucking me by the roots. He wanted to plant me into the beautiful garden of His great mercy and compassion.

He nurtured me like a tender shoot and fed me with true manna and watered me from the sweetest spring. And He protected me and forgave all my sins, and changed my address, for in lieu of hell, he gave me a home in the highest heaven.

That's why I will spend my life singing and testifying to the whole world that, in all the universe, there is none like Jesus. And for this reason I say to you that my gratitude is not like any other person's gratitude.

In this book, I will speak frankly about why I left Islam and why I followed Jesus.

I would like to begin with this passage of Scripture that the Apostle Paul wrote because it reminds me that even though I lost many things in this life, yet I have gained my Jesus, the lover of my soul.

> *Though I could have confidence in my own effort if anyone could. Indeed, if others have reason for*

confidence in their own efforts, I have even more! I was circumcised when I was eight days old. I am a pure-blooded citizen of Israel and a member of the tribe of Benjamin—a real Hebrew if there ever was one! I was a member of the Pharisees, who demand the strictest obedience to the Jewish law. I was so zealous that I harshly persecuted the church. And as for righteousness, I obeyed the law without fault. I once thought these things were valuable, but now I consider them worthless because of what Christ has done. Yes, everything else is worthless when compared with the infinite value of knowing Christ Jesus my Lord. For his sake I have discarded everything else, counting it all as garbage, so that I could gain Christ (Philippians 3: 4 - 8).

Jesus is the most beautiful thing in my life. And all that I have lost in this world, I consider but rubbish, thanking God that I know the Lord of lords and the King of kings who has dominion and power over all things.

I am writing, in this book, some of the important events of my life. I am writing them with simplicity, just as they happened.

Before I start my long story, I would like to tell you that "Rita" is not my real name but a nickname.

The journey of my life is the journey of exodus from failure, from loss, from selfishness, from the control of Satan, from sorrow, from darkness, from oppression, from fear, from weariness, from pride, from weakness, from loneliness, from evil and corruption.

The journey of my exodus is a crossing of various destinations. Each destination is a different stage unlike the one before it or the one after it.

Each stage is in a different country, followed by an exodus to the next country where the next stage occurs. That is what I will describe in detail to the best that my memory serves me of the past forty years.

I received the Lord Jesus Christ and testified that he was my Lord and Savior on July 15, 2002, and have spent the years since then carrying the cross and rising to the highest heaven through the path of blessedness, truth, and eternal life.

This path has cost me, and still does, much pain, separation, persecution, and severing of many family relationships with dear people that I loved and still love. But they have completely forsaken their relationships with me, just because I chose Jesus and followed his path.

I did not know that carrying the cross would cost me everything in my life, even things that had true value and held a special place in my heart and soul.

I could not imagine that, following Christ, I would have to give up everything that was dear to me. But, when I found that which is of greatest value, everything decreased its value in my eyes, and everything became worthless when I came to know the Lord Jesus.

Yet, in spite of all that I suffered, I thank the Lord that he rescued me, and saved me, and blessed me, and lifted me, and honored me with his name, and helped me to carry his cross. He strengthened me with his Word and crossed the oceans with me. He lit up my life and taught me, and is still teaching me how to live with him, for him, and under his favor. He changed me completely. He changed my thinking and my heart, and my thoughts and my dreams.

As I begin to write this book, I am watching the events of Najma Hamady in Egypt in January of 2010. Six young Christian men were killed as they were coming out of church after a Christmas service. Muslims killed them and the whole world joined the protests of the Coptic Christians in Egypt.

Also, just before this, there was a massacre in Baghdad at the church of Saida Alnajah. Believers were in the church praying when a group of criminals attacked them and killed many innocent people. Such news is painful and harsh, especially when it was perpetrated by Muslim fanatics.

Part I

Living
in the
Darkness

1

My Childhood

The Lord had a plan for my life from my early childhood. I only began to see that later on in my adult life. Now I see, as if I am looking at my life from above, that the Lord has guided my steps in exactly the order that he saw fit.

My father was a man full of strength, life, beauty and energy. He had a dominant personality and was faithful to his God till the end. He had 8 brothers and sisters who were my treasured aunts and uncles. My father inherited much of his personality from his own father Hajj Abdul Aziz, a powerful man who never put up with wrong, and had a great number of friends in the society at that time, in the southern part of Iraq where they lived in the city of Basra.

I did not see much of my grandfather, but in the few times I did see him, he was a strong, caring person who commanded the respect of everyone. Sadly, the circumstances of his death were tragic. He drowned while on a fishing trip with his friends and lost consciousness while diving into the sea. A great funeral was made for him when I was about 10 years old.

One of my earliest memories was when I was three years old. My father went to Cairo to study. My sister Azhar, my mother, and I went there with him. He went there to study the teachings of Islam at the University level. I remember the flat in which we lived in New Cairo, opposite the Metro station. Our neighbors had a boy and a girl, Mervatt and Amer, who were about my age. I still remember playing with them in the park and enjoying my time there very much.

However, not long after, my parents left me at my grandfather's house in Baghdad while they returned to Cairo. I had a wonderful time there and enjoyed the wonderful toys my parents sent me during holidays. It was a beautiful normal childhood without much talk about Islam. At least, at 3 years of age, I was unaffected by the religion.

Everyone we knew was Muslim and almost all were devoted to prayer and fasting according to the requirements of Islam. I was living with my grandparents and I used to watch my beautiful, smart, and wise grandmother who was full of personality, say her prayers. Everyone respected my grandmother and gave her honor. She was very wise in all her counsel. She loved me very much and let me sleep next to her while my parents were away in Egypt.

My grandmother used to pray the daily five prayers and read her Quran every day. I would see her wake up very early when it was

4

still dark and pray a prayer of blessing for her children. I used to watch her from under the blankets when she thought I was still asleep. Two of my aunts were sharing the room with us at that time. They have since passed into the afterlife. My grandmother would then get up and make breakfast for her sons and daughters because they were all studying at various universities. I had 5 uncles and 4 aunts and I was the only grandchild around, so I was loved and spoiled by everyone.

I don't know where my grandmother got her intelligence. She was a young widow and she raised ten children who all graduated from university. I don't know where she got her wisdom and how she managed to exercise authority over all her children. They all obeyed her and no one dared question her. The family was very religious, praying and fasting, and they were very polite and well mannered. They were not allowed to do anything but study, be around the house, and live a simple life. They used to read the Quran in a simple way. I have come to think that they did not understand what they read.

As for my beloved father, God bless him, he used to love his God in a great way. From the moment my eyes were opened in this world, I saw him pray. At first, his religion had no effect on me, but as I grew up, he became more fanatical in his religious devotion. When I was 6 years old, he casually started teaching me to pray. This was after he had finished his schooling in Egypt and returned to Iraq. Slowly, he began to teach me more and more about Islam.

When I turned seven, he became very serious about it. He used to quote something from the Prophet, which said, "Teach them when they are six, but beat it into them when they are seven." My father loved the Prophet Muhammad very much and used to quote him word for word. (Note: The Prophet refers to the Islamic prophet Muhammad throughout this book.)

I was the oldest of the three children, so I was the first one to be taught the ways of my father's religion. He taught me the proper way to pray and ceremonial washing. I had to wash, my hands, my mouth, my nose, and my face. I had to wipe down my head and ears and arms to the elbows and my feet with great care. While we washed we used to say certain verses. For example, when we washed the face, we would say, "O God, make my face shine in the day when faces will shine and do not make my face darkness in the day when faces will be darkened." When we washed our hands, we would say, "O God, give me my writing on my right side and not on my left side." When we wiped the hair, we would say, "O God, save my hair from the fires of hell."

He began to teach me the short and easy suras of the Quran by heart and even how to memorize the longer chapters. As for prayer, he used to stand in front of me and say, "Do exactly what I'm doing," especially during the prayers of dusk and night.

My memory of my mother at that time, however, was that she used to pray because she was supposed to, but she was not as devoted to religion as she is now.

2

Saudi Arabia

It is called the *kingdom* of Saudi Arabia because it is ruled by a king. This Muslim kingdom is full of every kind of adultery, sin, hard heartedness, corruption, and murder. The nature of the people of that land resembles the nature of the desert of that land- hard and empty of compassion and love.

When I was seven and eight years old, my parents took me along with my brother and sister to live in Saudi Arabia where my father had received a teaching contract. My mother also got a job as an elementary school teacher in a very small village. I was in the 2nd grade then.

In our first week there, my father took me with him to the market. And, as he took me with him, he was stopped by several men who asked him why his daughter was not wearing long clothes and covering her hair. My father, who was a devoted Muslim man, was very ashamed and began to feel that he should follow the

7

way of Islam fully. And, indeed, as soon as we got home, he ordered my mother to sew me a long dress that went down to the feet so that I can look like the young Saudi girls. From then on, I never left the house unless I was wearing one of the long dresses my mom, who was an outstanding seamstress, sewed for me.

My mother was an art teacher in the very same school that I attended. I was the only student from Iraq and was considered a foreigner like all other students who came from other countries. We were treated differently because we were outsiders.

The bus used to come daily to pick us up. My mother went out dressed like all the rest of Saudi women, covered from top to bottom by a black tent. The veil that covered her face was see-through, so she could see from behind it. All the women who were in the bus were dressed the same way. But, since I was only a child of seven, I was allowed to wear the long dress without covering my head. However, I was just about the only girl who didn't cover her head. The other little girls who were my age also walked around with their hair covered.

In the 2nd grade, each day, I had six periods of class. The first three periods were studying the Quran and theology. The last three periods were reserved for learning language, math and science. Thus we were required to study all matters that had to do with the Muslim religion including proper behavior and living at peace. At the same time, they taught the little children a love for Jihad for the sake of Islam and the love of fighting for the cause. We also had to memorize large portions of the Quran without understanding what it said. And I felt that Islam was filling me with fear and with the hardness of a soldier.

It was, of course, a girls' school called First School. All schools were ranked by their size and status. The best school was First

School, etc. As foreigners, we were put in First School and it covered all grades from first to twelfth.

The older girls, who were in high school, used to behave in strange ways that caught my attention as they would huddle together in a room. This made me curious and I sneaked a look to watch them. What I saw was shocking to me and terrified me but I could not get it out of my mind. They were touching each other in inappropriate ways.

From time to time there would be parties in one of the homes and all the women would be together. Believe me, on those occasions, I never heard a single mention of God. The parties were just an excuse to eat to the point of gluttony.

My father used to go five times a day to the mosque to pray. This was a requirement for all men. And when the bells chimed in the mosque, all public places and all the stores would close. Life just stopped. And if there was a man walking the streets at that time, he would be subjected to humiliation from the faithful men who watched people during prayer and beat them with sticks if they did not perform the requirements of the religion.

As for Fridays, that's when the main big prayers occurred and every man was required to attend. No man was allowed to stay in his house. My father used to come home after prayers full of sad and upsetting stories. He would tell us about the robbers that were caught the previous week and how they paraded them in the town square with all the men of prayer gathered around them quoting the Quran and saying, "As for those who steal, cut off their hands and do not show them any mercy or compassion."

And indeed, they obeyed the Quran without even the compassion of covering the eyes of those robbers. Then one of the butchers would come with a long knife or sharp sword and, making the men put their hands on a piece of wood, they would chop off their hand without mercy, and the street would swim with blood. All those men of prayer, seeing what happened to these robbers, would never dare to steal anything. When my father would tell us these stories, I would tremble with fear and would have nightmares about the blood streaming down the street.

Friday was the most dreaded day of the week for me—a day of evil and painful news, because the men who went to the mosque on Fridays would be exhorted to be more harsh and strict with their wives and daughters.

All of these matters would dig deeply into my brain. I can't imagine that after all this time, I still remember such vivid details.

I never saw any love in Saudi Arabia or any kind of tenderness, not from a teacher or any person anywhere. In fact, I used to count the days when I would go back to Iraq. My brother and sister and I would cry each day from confinement, and Mother would tell us to be patient because the year was almost over and we would never return to Saudi Arabia again. There was no place for fun there. Our only entertainment was to be with a few families from Iraq, Syria, and Lebanon who, like us, found themselves in Saudi Arabia in order to improve their finances. People only came there to make money. There, we had no museums or gardens or any beautiful things that a person can remember with fondness later. The only memories from that place were disturbing and upsetting.

During this period of time, my father continued to teach me how to pray in a proper manner. He also continued to teach me to memorize the Quran. In fact, since children have a greater ability to memorize things, I memorized some long and difficult sections.

The Muslims who came to Saudi Arabia from other Arab countries did not grow spiritually. The spiritual life of Islam is nothing more than empty rituals of right behavior. Many Muslims return to their countries hating Islam.

The Hajj

My family and friends consider me as someone who has completed the Hajj pilgrimage. This is a distinction in Islam. When I was 7 years old, I went with my parents to the Hajj. At that time I didn't understand anything. My mother sewed long beautiful white dresses for us that we call in Iraq a "dushdasha." We rode in a large station wagon that is designed to carry luggage in the back, but we sat in the back. When we arrived in Mecca, we fulfilled the required rituals. With my mother, I walked 7 times around the Kaaba. We also walked the long path from Safa to Marwa 7 times.

Although I did not understand anything I was doing, I have a vivid memory of some of the things I saw there. I remember we went to the place where Satan is battled. I was very afraid even though I was with my family among many people. There were many cars, big and small, and massive numbers of people arriving there at sunset. People were throwing little stones at a building standing from a distance. This house had two stories and the lights inside were on. I was very afraid and imagined the devil was really living in that house. This memory terrified me and haunted me for a long time.

I remember also that the people were most interested in shopping. One time a taxi took us from our hotel to the Harum

(Mosque). My father said to the taxi driver, "I envy you because you live in the blessed city of Mecca, and you are close to the house of God and you always come there to pray." The taxi driver said in all honesty, "I have lived in Mecca all my life and I never visited the Harum, not even once, and I never walked around the Kaaba."

The mercies of God

I remember once, if it were not for the mercy of God, I would have been raped. In the first year of our stay in Saudi Arabia, I was seven years old and we were living in a small flat. In front of our house there was another small flat where a man and his wife lived, and their children used to play with us. One day, my father was out of the house in the Mosque and my mother was visiting with this lady. All of us children were on the roof where we used to hang out in the late afternoon, because there were no parks for us to play in, and even if there were parks, women were not allowed to be there.

My mother called out to me to go fetch something from our house. As I was coming down, the husband of the woman who was visiting with my mother saw me and said, "Come on, child, come in here, I want to give you some chocolate." As soon as I walked into his house, he closed the door. Immediately I heard my father coming up the stairs and I opened the door and ran out. My father saw me coming out of this man's home. His face dropped and he sternly asked me, "What are you doing in there?" I told him that the man had called me. My father beat me and told me very sternly, "You must stay with your mother and never go out of her sight." My father also scolded the man fiercely and

12

cut off all relationship between us and that family. This made me very afraid of men.

After the school year was over, we returned to Iraq. But we returned the next school year to Saudi Arabia, to a different village called Ha'el. That year was just as awful as the year before. Those two years of my life made a lasting impression on me, so that after all these years, I still remember things quite vividly. But I believe that this was always the will of God for me from the beginning.

3

Iraq

I remember when I came out of the airplane to my beloved country of Iraq, I knelt down and kissed the ground. Even though I was just a child, I felt the value of my sweet home after living in a place where nothing was allowed, and everyone disliked outsiders and treated them badly.

I remained in Iraq throughout my elementary and secondary school years and I attended university there as well. That meant that I lived my entire youth in the shadow of Islam because every single member of my family and friends were Muslim.

When I returned from Saudi Arabia, at the age of eight, I started the fourth grade with quite a good amount of knowledge about the teachings of Islam. I had memorized much more of the Quran than the Iraqi children my age. This made my father very happy and, every time a guest came to visit, my father would make me recite what I had learned.

In my fourth grade class, religion classes were just once a week whereas in Saudi Arabia they were every day. In those times, Iraq was not a very religious nation. The religion book we had in school was very minimal and it had some of the suras of the Quran with the meanings of the words and explanations about ceremonial washing. For me, this was very very easy because I had had a lot of advanced study. Sometimes I even corrected the teacher in what she was explaining.

One day the teacher told me, "Why don't you come, child, and explain some of the things you learned in Saudi Arabia." So, every week I stood in front of the students and taught the religion class instead of the teacher, as she had requested. I explained to them the methods of washing and prayer.

As I grew up and went to junior high and high school, I began to ask my father many questions regarding religion. For example, "Why does Islam allow a man to marry up to four wives?" But my father's answers did not satisfy me. He said, "This is what God has ordained. And He did it for the sake of the woman so she can have a home and be protected because it is wrong for a woman to be without a husband." I did not understand why it was wrong for a woman to not have a husband. I did not understand why it was better to be a fourth wife to a man who already had three before her, than to be single.

My father and the Muslim Brotherhood

As a family, we began to have problems with my father because he made the acquaintance of some Muslim brothers. This changed him completely. He became a man with a hard heart and sharp words. I began to feel that he no longer loved us. Peace

15

left our house and in its place there was shouting and sorrow. All of a sudden, everything was forbidden.

We began to fear our father and wish he would stay in the Mosque and not return home each night. One Friday, he came home after the prayers seeming very bothered by something. When my mother asked him what was wrong, he said, "I have not been doing what God wants. I didn't really know what he wanted, but now I do. From this moment on, I must never touch your sisters." My mother asked, "What happened to you?" He said, "There is a noble saying of the Prophet Muhammad, 'If your head is sewn by a thread made of iron, it's better for you not to touch a woman that does not belong to you.'" My mother replied, "This is humiliating. We're one family and all of them respect you and love you." But he replied, "I must obey my God." She then asked, "And what about our neighbors and friends? How will they understand this?" His answer came clearly out of what he had been taught by the Sheik in the Mosque, "Put your hands on your sides and by this the woman will know that you do not want to shake hands with her. Or put your hands on your chest so that the sister will know that you do not want to touch her with your hands."

And this is what my father started to do with my aunts, explaining it all to them. He also taught my brother Ahmed not to shake hands with my friends and female cousins. He would tell him, "Try to stand far away from a woman so you do not have to shake her hands, or look at the floor so she doesn't come over and greet you."

And he really did follow this rule from that day on because he wanted to please his God in everything he did. So, when my aunt came to visit, and tried to greet him, he would not touch her and he told her that from now on he would not do so because it was forbidden. He also forbad us from greeting our male cousins even though we had up to then lived with them like brothers and sisters. In fact, he planted ideas and thoughts in our minds that we would not have had if he hadn't forbidden everything.

The following Friday, my father again came home angry and this time it was because my sister and I were not wearing the hijab. I hated the hijab and would have rather died than wear it because I was very much into wearing fashionable clothing. So, there was fighting and anger in our household. I begged my mother to talk to my father and tell him I did not like nor did I want to wear these clothes. My mother wanted very much to keep us happy especially since she, herself, was not devoted to the Muslim religion. She did however pray the prayers and read the Quran even though she did not understand it.

The matter was settled by my dad and he forbad me to leave the house without wearing the hijab. So, I covered my head and went to school, but I was very upset about it. So, I would wear the hijab in front of my father because I was afraid of him, but when he was not around, I took it off.

My father never sat down with me to explain to me why I should cover my head. He never sat down to explain to me anything about God. Who is God? Does this God love me or not? I knew nothing about this God and I had no relationship with him, neither a distant one, nor a close one. And I could see that my father and mother did not know why they worshipped God.

Fridays became dreaded days for us. My father would return home after the Friday prayers with a somber countenance and he wouldn't want to speak to us. We knew in our hearts that there was some big matter that was bothering him as usual. At around 2 in the afternoon, we would all gather to eat but we wouldn't say a word. We were afraid to ask him what was wrong. My sweet mother would try to smile at him and ask him if he liked the dinner. But he would not reply to any questions. It seemed that even the food was not to his liking. He would wait till after dinner to start his lecture.

This particular time, he started talking about television, saying that it was shameful, and that it was especially shameful to watch music shows and Arabic movies. He then forbad us from ever watching movies or else he would actually break the TV set so we could never watch anything. Of course this was a very difficult problem for us, especially for my younger sister Azhar, because she loved watching television, especially Arabic movies. TV was just about our only breath of fresh air because we hardly went anywhere except for an occasional visit to my aunts.

Watching television became one of our difficulties especially since we had some shows that we liked and movies that we absolutely loved. My mother also loved movies, but she did not dare go against her husband's wishes. She knew it was wisest for her to obey him. My father would go to sleep very early each night and we did not know how we could watch TV behind his back without him seeing us or hearing us. We knew if he woke up suddenly to go to the bathroom and saw the lights on in the living room and the TV on, we would have a giant problem.

We wanted so badly to watch an Arabic movie. It was Thursday night and they always had a new movie on that night and we loved staying up to watch it because the next day we had no school. So, my sister Azhar and I decided to sit in the living room with the lights off and put the volume on the TV to its lowest level. My brother and youngest sister were asleep in bed. We had one other problem to solve and that is, the light from the TV might show under the closed door. If our father saw that and found us, he would treat us like criminals. So, we decided to put a blanket at the bottom of the door so when he woke up he would see only darkness.

So, my sister and I were ready for this deception. We waited in our room until our father finished listening to the news from London as he always did and then went to bed. Before he went to bed, he always checked to see if we were all in our rooms and that no one was in the living room. When we were sure he was in his room, my sister and I sneaked out quietly to the living room and laid the blanket at the bottom of the door. We turned on the TV and started watching our movie. Inside, we were terrified as if we had committed a terrible crime—the crime of watching an Arabic movie in our home.

We had one ear on the movie and another waiting to hear if my dad opened his door. After a short while, we heard the door open. My sister and I were terrified and we jumped up and turned off the TV. I told my sister, "Let's hide behind the door or behind the curtain, so if he opened the door, he would see no one in the room and the TV off." But he went to the bathroom and returned to his room without opening the living room door. My heart was pounding in my chest and my knees were knocking together. I finally talked my sister into forgetting the TV and going to bed. We knew if he found us out we would be in deep trouble. So, we went to bed.

The next day was Friday and we were afraid of whatever new teaching that would descend on us. But my father came in accusing us of neglecting our religious studies and especially of

19

not waking up early enough to pray the morning prayers. He also was angry that we had not memorized the names of God and that our prayers were too fast and we were not praying properly. We had failed him in so many ways, it seemed.

After lunch, my father went into his bedroom to take a short nap before the afternoon prayers. My sister was watching TV and I don't remember whether or not she was watching any of the forbidden movies or music programs. The living room door was open and my father's bedroom door was across the hall from the living room. When he woke up and saw the television on, he silently went into the storage room where he kept his tools and he brought a large heavy hammer, and with a look full of anger and hate, he began to smash the television screen until the TV was just a rubble of small fragments strewn all over the room.

My sister started screaming and crying and I ran out of my room when I heard the commotion. Seeing my sister crying and the horrible scene in front of me, I began to cry too. My mother was yelling in my father's face, "What you're doing is wrong, it's not good." But my father was yelling back, "I warned all of you and promised you that I would break the television and you did not listen and obey!"

Every Friday, we began to expect some great problem that my father would bring with him when he came back from the mosque.

As more and more things became forbidden and more and more rules were added to us, I began to hate Islam and to hate wearing the horrible coverings. Everything had to be done by rules. We had to eat only with our right hand. If we wanted to take a drink, you had to take it in three sips, never one time like the animals. We had to wake up and pray before the sun came up or else our prayers wouldn't be heard.

When our relatives came to visit us, we had to cover our heads and the women had to sit in a separate room from the men. My father would always tell us a woman is sin which meant I was sin and I had to cover up from my head to the bottom of my feet in order to cover up the sin. I truly began to hate my life. I kept hearing everywhere I went that I was sin and there was no escape. There was no hope of life ever having any happiness.

4

Jordan

The next few years of my life continued to be very difficult and dark years. But eventually, I was able to leave Iraq and go to Jordan, a small, beautiful and clean country that imprinted many good and unforgettable memories on my heart.

In Jordan, I saw many women covering their heads in the streets. But their head coverings were stylish and alluring. And the dresses that the women wore covered everything but they were tightly fitting dresses and very suggestive. However, from the Muslim rules point of view, their heads were covered and that's all that mattered. They were fulfilling the letter of the law. They were respected more than me because my head was not covered, although my clothes were much more modest than theirs. Having your hair uncovered is considered a great indiscretion in Islam.

What caught my attention in Jordan, especially in summer, was the great number of people who came from Saudi Arabia or the gulf countries to spend their vacations in Jordan. They would come in their fancy cars with their wives and daughters all covered up, but they would sit with these covered up women in restaurants and look at all the other women. And those who left their wives in the hotels or back home, would come to the cafés and restaurants and would stare lustfully at the women. This was not only obvious to me, but to everyone. Jordan was very European compared to the countries these tourists came from.

At that time, Jordan was full of great numbers of Iraqi people who had escaped from the hard political struggles in Iraq. They were seeking a safe refuge and Jordan was a beautiful, safe country, full of people from many different places. Everyone who came to Jordan found what he needed. The devout Muslim could find there a plethora of Muslim people and Mosques. The devout Christian could likewise find there a plethora of Christian people and churches from every denomination. And the person who cared nothing for any religion could do what he wanted without interference from anyone.

Since Jordan is centrally located in the Arab world, it's a place where people from all over the Middle East converge. It's a country surrounded by other countries that have had great political upheavals, like Iraq, Palestine and Israel. Nevertheless, this unique country has managed to maintain its peace and beauty and cleanliness. And the people of Jordan are kind and caring. And I was touched by their kindness and peacefulness.

I got to know some Christian friends in Jordan. They were sweet people who truly loved me with a pure love, and didn't care that my family and I were Muslims. They introduced me to the Christian life by their actions. They used to have a prayer meeting every Tuesday for the believers, and they invited my family as well. I attended their meetings with my sister and approximately ten Christian families. We enjoyed their spiritual songs, and then we listened to their Bible study without really understanding. My sister went with me but when she heard them saying Jesus was the Son of God she objected and said, "God forgive them. They are denying God! God was not born and has no sons." She begged me to get out of that house. But I stopped her because I didn't want to miss out on those holy moments.

I used to feel comfortable in these meetings in spite of my disagreement with their beliefs. I said to myself that they had their own religion and we had ours, and they were pitiable but simple and good hearted people. Their praises were calm and quiet, and their relationships with each other were full of love, kindness, forgiveness, and peace. I used to love this atmosphere but without getting deeply involved with them because I didn't want to dive into a false religion which was not my own.

This experience made me turn more to God and devote myself to praying for very long hours in the morning and evening, because I noticed that God listened to my prayers. I know now that I was simple and superficial in my faith, because I was concentrating my prayers on my personal and financial needs.

In fact, when I lived in Jordan, I began to devote myself more and more to Islam. I learned to pray for long hours, praying to a God that I didn't know. I stayed on the prayer mat for long periods of time, especially between the sunset and the dinner prayers when I read the Quran. My father pushed us often to pray and read the Quran. He used to tell us, "Whoever reads from the Quran is not reading by tongue only, but all of the body parts are reading too, and every cell of the blood is reading too." My motivation for reading the Quran came from his words and also from the idea that reading the Quran for long periods of time earned favor with God. We were taught that the only way to enter heaven was to earn enough positive favor with God.

I didn't know, because Islam doesn't have this teaching, that God loved me. I never even thought of wondering whether or not God loved me. Love didn't enter my mind, but I did notice something tangible, which is that when I prayed to him and asked him for something, he often granted my requests. So I continued praying for him to get me out of the hard times I was living in, and to help me find work so I can make a living without depending on anybody.

Amazingly, God answered me and I found work as an art teacher in one of the big private high schools. Getting the job made me feel that God was actually with me, because I reached a very good position in the school and a very good income which helped me to pay the rent and the other expenses.

My experience at Al-Orouba School

I would like to share a special experience I had at Al-Orouba School. This experience made me become more devoted to Muslim prayer. The school was a distinguished school with fine buildings, a good location, and an exceptional educational reputation. Most of the teachers, the superintendent and his assistant were Christians. The school contained all the grades from the elementary level up to high school.

The principal of the high school, whose name was Huda, was a generous woman, very sophisticated, and with a high degree of integrity. She was modest and had a charismatic personality. I will never forget her goodness to me. This great woman helped me to find a job, and stood by me in time of need. When she found that I lived near to her, she started to pick me up in the morning and take me home after school. Huda was a Muslim woman but she was a simple Muslim woman who didn't wear the head covering. When she received a lot of blame from the Muslim teachers who were covering their heads, she used to reply calmly that she would think about it. She behaved with a righteous heart and dealt fairly and kindly with others. In turn, she earned the respect and affection of others.

I was the Art Teacher for the high school level but I had a lot of trouble with the students at the beginning. I tend to have a serious temperament, while the Art subject is not considered a serious subject, and the students wanted to enjoy themselves and goof around in my class. It was hard for me to control the class and keep it calm. Furthermore, I was in a probationary period to prove my qualifications to be hired permanently at the school. The students were from rich families and spoiled; therefore, I had to be wise in my behavior towards them, making sure not to hurt anybody's feelings or talk to them in a way that would get me in big trouble.

I would come home and complain to my mother and she would pray for me. I would kneel on the prayer mat long into the night, and wake up in the early morning while it was still dark to pray with tears. I wanted God to give me ideas and strength to help me overcome my problems at school. I prayed that I would be able to motivate the students and make them like my Art Class.

God was with me and gave me a great idea which I implemented. I told my students that if they kept quiet in class, I would take them out on a journey to the mountains to draw out in nature. At the same time I arranged with the principal to schedule one of the school busses for me and the students to go out for a field trip. I took the first class to one of the mountain areas in Amman, and we sat on rocks, drew pictures and collected rocks to make a nature display inside the school. The girls had so much fun and by the end of the day, when we went back to school, I was so grateful to God because that day was different from all of the previous days.

I didn't know that the news of my fieldtrip had spread to the whole school. When I entered another class the next day, I was surprised that all of the students were polite and unusually quiet. While I was wondering at this change, one of the girls asked me, "Are you going to take us on a fieldtrip like you did with the other class, especially since we are silent and behaving very well today?" I smiled and said, "For sure," and I took them later on a fieldtrip to an Art Exhibit. So, in time, the Art class became one of the most enjoyable and important lessons for the students, and all the students started to do their best to keep me satisfied.

The principal heard the news from the students and was happy because she was the one who hired me. After that she asked me to make an art gallery display at the school. This would be an important event for the Art department in the school, and accordingly this would affect my permanent position.

I was quite worried, and didn't know where to begin. My mother also could see that I was worried, and she prayed for me, because by now, she was a praying woman. She used to wake up in the middle of the night before the dawn to pray. I asked her to wake me with her, and I started to pray to God to give me an idea for the gallery.

He did! He inspired me with an idea of how to decorate the office they gave me and the hallway and display the students' art work there.

The idea was to collect rocks and put them in front of the wall and draw seas and ships on the wall. The next day, with the principal's permission, I took one of the classes and started to collect rocks from the mountain. I also bought big buckets of wall paint. I had the talented students draw sea waves along with ships and fish on the hallway wall. Since the art gallery date was getting closer, we started to work every day after school so we could finish the display on time.

A disaster at work

One day, there were a lot of students working, each on a part of the wall. They were really enjoying what they were doing until one of the students accidentally dropped a can of blue paint on the floor! I didn't have enough rags or papers to clean the floor, but we tried. The problem was that the paint was an oil based paint and so it needed an alcohol based solvent to remove it. I didn't know what to do. I couldn't be angry with the girl that dropped the paint because it was an accident and she was voluntarily working with me during her after school hours.

The students saw the pain on my face but they didn't know how to help. Now, instead of progressing on the gallery, we started to clean the beautiful ground that was trashed. At that moment I truly wished that I had never gotten that job at the school. I was sure that I would soon be fired.

We finally had to give up and go home. The hallway was a mess and I couldn't sleep that night. I had a terrible dream that the next day everyone showed up at school and was shocked at the condition of the hallway. No one could walk on it because it was slippery. I dreamt that the principal called me in and turned me over for an investigation. They fined me a great deal of money to pay for the cleaning. I couldn't pay the fine, so they turned me into the police and threw me in jail.

I woke up and cried because I didn't know how I would face the principal who had always supported me. The next morning was Saturday, so I woke up early and started to cry to God and beg him to have mercy on me. When I got to school, the principal had seen the tragic situation. The science teacher's room was the first room in the hallway. She claimed that the slippery ground would endanger her students. In addition the color would stick to their shoes and would dirty the science lab. Moreover, the stinky oily smell was everywhere.

My principal was also distressed but she treated me with a great deal of respect. She offered to buy the cleaning materials but I would have to clean the floor. I was so relieved because I felt that God was with me and he was supporting me. I thanked him so much from the bottom of my heart for the tenderness that he put in the principal's heart.

I started to do my best to clean every day. I stayed long hours at school along with some of my students who loved me and got their parents' permission to stay. Each day we cleaned till we were totally exhausted. Then I would go home and pray and pray for help from God. Through our hard work, God had his hand on us and the ground became clean and beautiful.

Finally, we got back to working on the gallery. The day was getting very near, only two weeks away. I asked the principal to take a look at what we had done, and she was surprised at how beautiful everything looked. On opening day the principal, the superintendent and the inspection committee came along with the teachers to look at the exhibit. Everyone was impressed.

The principal said proudly, "This Art teacher is Iraqi, and she's been here less than six months. She's been working late hours, and even on the weekends and holidays." This shows why I'm so proud to know this great woman. Through her, I received the gratitude and appreciation of the whole school. I was as happy as if I were in heaven, and returned home filled with joy. I knew that God responded to my mother's prayers and mine. I had a wish in my heart to know more about God's character and to get to know him personally, but this was impossible in my religion.

Leaving Jordan

I was very happy with the way things were going at Al-Orouba schools, but God had other plans for my life and began to put a great desire in my heart to leave Jordan and go to The Netherlands where my aunt was living.

It was not an easy thing to go to The Netherlands. I needed the proper visa and those visas were very hard to come by. Because of my experience at school, my relationship with God was getting much closer. I felt that God loved rewarding the long prayers and readings from the Quran. So I continued to read the Quran every day and pray for long periods of time for God to open the door for me to travel to The Netherlands. I would beg and plead and cry out in my prayers, thinking that through this kind of prayer I was forcing God to grant my request and facilitate my travel.

Each time I prayed, I would persist more and more and repeat the phrase, "My God, facilitate my travel to The Netherlands." I would wake up in the middle of the night and pray the Tajahod Prayer which is kneeling twice and demanding from God to facilitate my travel to The Netherlands.

At this period of my life, I started to become more religious, more like my beloved father. I started to go to the Mosque on Friday (King Abdulla Mosque) thinking that if I was nearer to God, he would be more pleased with me and more likely to grant my requests. Friday was considered a blessed day, and I had heard from my father that there was an hour in it when heaven opens its doors and the prayers would all be acceptable to God. No one knew when that hour was, so we had to pray all day, hoping to get our answer. So I decided on my own to keep insisting in my prayers for God to grant my desire.

I wasn't really following the teachings of Islam. I hadn't studied real Islamic teachings since my school days. I was holding on to a legacy I had learned from my beloved Father, so that I could manipulate God into doing what I wanted. What was required was for me to increase my prayer, fasting and reading the Quran even if I didn't understand it truly like other Muslim people did. The important thing was the quantity of time spent reading the Quran. The more I read, the more score went into the balance of my favors with God.

Understanding what I read was not important as I believed the blessing was in the *reading,* not *understanding* God's book, the Quran. I also knew I was required to do good works and pray five

31

times a day asking for what I needed in my life. Again I insisted, "God, facilitate my travel to Holland."

I didn't even know whether going there would be good for me or bad. So I was afraid to say to God, "If it is your will, please facilitate my travel." I thought that his will is to make us suffer or grieve us. It wasn't his will that mattered to me then. Only mine!

Surprisingly enough, God answered my prayer with a miracle. I actually got the required visa! I didn't know how long I would be able to stay in The Netherlands, therefore, I went to my principal and explained to her that I didn't know when I would be back again. She said, "It will be very hard to come back to your position if you leave it." Her words hurt me because I loved my work; I loved my principal, the students, the teachers and the workers, but this was my way out of Jordan and I wanted to take it.

Part II

Birth
of the
Holy Light

1

The Netherlands

The Lord Jesus said: "And I have other sheep that are not of this fold. I must bring them also, and they will listen to my voice. So there will be one flock, one shepherd" (John 10:16).

Consider these words of the apostle Paul:

I was advancing in Judaism beyond many of my own age among my people, so extremely zealous was I for the traditions of my fathers. But when he who had set me apart before I was born, and who called me by his grace (Galatians 1: 14 – 15).

I would like to restate the words of Paul and say, "I was advancing in Islam, but he who had set me apart before I was born, took me to The Netherlands."

I would consider this stage of my life the strongest and most fertile stage. It provided the foundation that I stand on now. This is where my real life started. Those eight years were unforgettable for many reasons. It was the first time I travelled to the West, the first time I lived alone and swam in hard waters. The first time I met someone who turned my life upside down from the roots. He is my endless love and my soul, the Lord Jesus Christ. I also had to learn a new language, but also, in my alienation, I lost my beloved father, Hajj Yahya Abdul-Aziz.

Yet the Lord was with me throughout this difficult journey. My astonishment was great at all levels. And I felt like a naïve child who didn't know how to walk or speak, like a blind woman who came from the depth of darkness into the blinding light so that I could hardly open my eyes to understand what was happening. The change was so complete in me; it was like I had been dead and brought back to life.

I found myself suddenly thrust away from family and relatives into a great field throbbing with people with different nationalities, languages and religions. I found myself dealing with large numbers of strangers of different races, colors, countries and languages.

I entered into The Netherlands because God helped me obtain a visa through my beloved aunt (whom I call Um Saad) who was living there at the time. My aunt unfortunately passed away from this world in November 2012.

When my aunt was living in Iraq, she was a common Muslim who didn't wear the head covering, so I was surprised, when I saw her in The Netherlands, that she had dived more deeply into Islam, wearing the head covering, praying regularly, and reading the

Quran and the religious books. She, her husband, and children were now fanatical Muslims. I didn't quite know why. But I guessed that my aunt was compelled to comply with her husband because she was required to be loyal to him in order to continue living with him in peace.

I found out that she and her husband were in very good standing with the militants Muslims in The Netherlands. It made me feel like I was still in a small uncivilized village, not in a civilized country. When I came from Jordan into their circle, I was at that time a Muslim but still not wearing the head covering. I did love God, or more precisely, I was worshipping God in honesty, as I had been raised in my father's house. I used to pray the five prayers (morning, noon, afternoon, sunset and dinner), and with each prayer I did two extra "kneels," according to Sunni teaching, before the prayer or after, according to what was required. My aunt and her husband also prayed all the prayers. My aunt was active in religious issues, and was loyal to the God that she was worshipping.

I lived near Rotterdam, near the city of Breda where my aunt lived. So, I used to go to visit her regularly, especially during the weekends. We did not talk about religious issues often, but we did love each other as family and my relationship with them was full of respect and love.

Family relationships in a foreign country were very important to me. They gave me a kind of safe and secure feeling of knowing that I had some relatives to turn to. My aunt was very generous and would make me highly nutritious food because she noticed how bad my financial situation was. She would also make special Middle Eastern desserts for me which she also did professionally.

I used to stay with them on Saturdays and Sundays and would leave them happy, having spent a good weekend with my only relatives in The Netherlands. My aunt would also give me what I needed whether it was money or food. This was happening every weekend, and I felt a kind of happiness and security when I was with them because I was connected to one of my relatives. I truly missed that later when I became like an enemy to them.

The Lord Jesus knows the heart of each person. He knew that my weakness was my desire for a strong connection to my family. And when he brought me back to the true God, the Lord Jesus, he led me away from my family, my country, and my traditions. He had to remove me from under the tight control of the Islamic atmosphere, especially since I was alone as a powerless Islamic woman.

When I was among my family it was impossible to think except in Islamic terms, but when I was alone in a foreign country, the Lord Jesus was able to show me who I really was, and touch my life, and remove me from the influence of Islam.

Since I was young, I was thought to be a stubborn child. My family thought that I was strong, but my stubbornness or my strength was only external. I looked strong from the outside, but on the inside I was a very weak person with no strength or personality to face hard situations. Moreover, my feelings were easily hurt by the slightest word. I was so sensitive that my tears would flow when I saw anybody in pain or sick or even poor. I cried when my heart was moved by stories of people going through hard time, or when I remembered a sad memories or people that I had lost.

I say this because, though I was happy when I was with the family on the weekends, I was overwhelmed with the rest of life.

Life in the refugee camp

I lived in a refugee camp in a small village in The Netherlands called Krimpen A/D Ijssel in the district of the city of Rotterdam. It was a small hotel located on a very small lake in a beautiful place. This place was not selected by me but by God, for me. The village was full of churches of many different Christian denominations, and there were a lot of true believers filled with the Holy Spirit and God's love, eager to share the Word of the Lord Jesus.

I lived in the camp with a large group of people, some of whom were families and some singles. At first I lived with three women in a small room on the third floor. We were three Muslims and one Christian, each worshipping alone. One of the Muslim women was an elderly woman. She used to wake up early before daybreak while it was still dark. One day, I asked her to wake me up when she awoke. She was surprised by my request because she didn't know that I was from an Islamic family, but she started to wake me up to pray before sunrise. I would pray, then read some of the Quran, though, in all honesty, I did not understand it, and then I would go back to sleep until almost nine in the morning. At that time, I had only been in The Netherlands a few short months and didn't have a job or school. Our Christian roommate used to pray her Christian prayers, and from time to time during the night we would discuss the issue of heaven and hell. We realized that, as for me and the other Muslim women, we didn't know where we would be spending our eternal life.

In fact, we didn't know much about Islam, and didn't understand the meaning of most Quran verses, in spite of our daily readings. Our knowledge of the Quran was simple. The Christian woman had been born to Christian parents and she revered the Lord Jesus and Mother Mary a lot, but, I don't think she had a personal relationship with the Lord Jesus at that time.

My living circumstances were hard at that time from all aspects. I lived in a small room, with four women, and didn't know what my destiny would be or how long we would all stay in this situation. It was a life of waiting. We slept and ate in the same room. We had to share the restroom with others. Everyone came from a different family background, culture, and tradition, yet we still had to live day and night together, with every detail of life, such as a phone call, lived in front of each other. In this way we were forced to know the details of each others' lives.

The room was so small that there was room for only three beds, so I was forced to sleep on the floor because I was the last one to come and live with them. In the place where we could have put a fourth bed, we had our only table. I was forced to accept whatever happened to me because I was in a foreign country and had no recourses. So I agreed to sleep on the floor so we could have the benefit of a table to eat and write on. When I tried to go to the management of the hotel to ask for a transfer to a larger room, they refused, because the law was very strict, and the refugees were required to accept everything.

Life was difficult with my roommates. For example, the old woman, who was waking me up to pray, would go into the bathroom to take a bath and spend a lot of time inside. We were always waiting to use the toilet or wash our hands or drink the water. One of the women couldn't handle heat, and wanted to keep the door and the window always open. She needed cold weather to be able to function, but I was the opposite. I wanted to be in a warm place and couldn't handle the cold, especially since I was so slim. So I would be shaking all the time in the freezing Netherlands' weather. If I closed the door or the window, my roommate would go and open them again. People in The Netherlands always close their doors and turn on the heaters to get warm. But I was always sitting on the ground with the covers on me to try to shake off the cold.

The days were passing slowly and my sense of humiliation was growing, away from the family in a foreign country, no light of hope in my situation, a deep sense of loss, and a fear that I was heading for big trouble. I couldn't go back, and there was no positive progress. All the doors seemed closed, and therefore the only thing I could do was to become more devoted to prayer. Prayer was my only entertainment and for a long time I would pray to God to open some doors. I didn't know where to go. I wondered if my stay in this country was from God. Should I continue in this painful and annoying life or go back to my family or what? I had plenty of puzzling questions, and no one there to help me, and no way to be saved from my miserable life.

This life is what I had been dreaming of and wishing for when I was in Jordan. I had prayed to God to open the door to me to come to The Netherlands, and he had responded to me. I was now in the most beautiful country in the world, an elegant country, full of roses with lovely colors, marvelous lakes full of slim white swans, swimming calmly and peacefully. Ducks and birds walked freely among the people and without any fear of being hunted. There's an amazing freedom in this country, but in spite of all of this freedom, I was feeling the chains on me. I could certainly not enjoy any of this freedom because the feeling of alienation, heaviness and pain were overwhelming me. The only thing that kept me going was that everyone around me had the same feelings. Of course each of us was feeling that our own pain was the greatest and the hardest, so I would cry a lot, but when I called my family I wouldn't tell them about my pains and sadness.

I used to sit for long hours reading the Quran, especially Surat Al-Wakiah. I read it 40 times in one session because it was supposed to open the doors of livelihood. It took at least three hours to finish it. I also spent 4 hours reading Surat Yassin 40 times because I had heard that if I read it 40 times in a row, I would receive a miracle. This was the extent of my faith. It was based on manipulating God to get what I wanted, so I believed that one day I would have an answer from God.

I meet a "defector"

One day, a Russian woman who lived in the room opposite mine knocked at my door and invited me to come with her to an American church. She said, "Why are you always in the room crying and being sad and lonely in your alienation? Come with me to the church where you can meet people who speak your Arabic language."

I agreed and went with her to church. I didn't understand the sermon or the songs, even though they were in English, which I knew a little bit. It was all so new and different to me. After the service I met an Arab whom my neighbor had told me about. He introduced himself to me as Abdul Kader from Algeria. When I heard his name and the country, I asked with excitement, "It means you are Muslim?"

He said he used to be a Muslim. So, I asked him, "And now what? Are you a Christian?" When he said yes, the color on my face changed immediately. It was like he had slapped me in the face. I was absolutely shocked. It was the first time in my life that I had heard about someone leaving the great religion of Islam. I started to look at him in a cynical and sarcastic way, and asked him in a degrading way, as if I could never believe that there is a human being in this world who would even think of leaving the true Islamic religion, "This means you left your religion, your family and became Christian?"

He humbly said yes with a smile. And when he said that, I felt he was a disgusting person. I went back to my room in the camp thinking of this person who had left his religion and become a Christian. I felt proud and happy that I was a devout Muslim. I determined in my heart to start talking about Islam to all those poor deluded people who were headed for hell. And when I reached my room, I performed the ritual ablution and prayed the noon and afternoon prayers and read the Quran until it was time for the sunset prayer.

My introduction to Jesus

By the end of seven months, two of my roommates had left The Netherlands to another country. The Christian woman's family had arrived so they lived together in one room, and I lived on the ground floor in the same building with another of their daughters.

I felt like I was part of this family. I felt the same love and the tenderness with them that I felt with my real family. They were a mother, father, two daughters and three sons. We ate and drank together daily and they were always respectful of my Islamic religion. I continued to worship with reverence in my daily prayers and continued the Quran reading while at the same time living like one of the members of this Christian family. In the morning we were busy going to the Dutch language school, after that we ate, did our washing and cleaning, or ran errands. In the evening I prayed my regular Islamic prayers that I had learned since childhood, then I did my Quran reading, then I sat with the family watching them pray their ritual Christian prayers which were so totally different from my prayers.

They had a small book that they would read some beautiful words out of, and then they would repeat some prayers using the Rosary Rosette. I started asking them about these prayers. I wondered how they could pray without first doing the ritual washings. They said that God looks at the heart. They said they took baths every day and had clean clothes, so there was no need for ablutions. Then they opened the Holy Bible, and started to read to me about Jesus. They said he was not an ordinary person, that he performed miracles by a touch of his hand, or by a word from his mouth, that he was alive and didn't die.

I remember one night they read the story of Jesus going down from the mountain and meeting a leprous man, (which is a skin disease with spots on the skin). This was a contagious disease and accordingly the person who had this disease was considered very infectious and had to be quarantined. Nobody was allowed to come near him, not even his family because there was no cure for this disease. This leper must have been suffering psychologically and physically, with all the people in his life shunning him due to his disease, but when he heard that Jesus has the ability to heal, he found Jesus and knelt at his feet begging, "Lord, if you want you can make me clean."

I was surprised when they said that Jesus touched him with his hand and healed him. Again Jesus entered into one of his disciple's homes where his mother in law was sick with a fever. Jesus also touched her hand and the fever left her and she got up to serve them. Later that night he cast out many evil spirits. I was listening carefully to these beautiful stories, and being really touched by Jesus' goodness. These discussions were really affecting me and making me full of questions. We kept awake that night till late hours talking.

We agreed to continue our discussion the next day. So, the next night, after I finished my prayers, I went to their room opposite mine and found them praying. After the prayer, we continued the discussion about Jesus' miracles. They told me the story of feeding the five thousand with only five loaves of bread and two fishes (Matthew 14:13 – 21). This miracle surprised me, especially that there were 12 baskets full of leftovers.

Another time Jesus and his disciples got into a boat and a great storm arose while Jesus was sleeping in the boat. The disciples woke up Jesus crying, "Lord we are dying." Then Jesus calmed the wind and the sea with just a word and the disciples were surprised and said, "Who is this person that the wind and the sea obey him?" (Matt 8:23 – 27). I felt the same way as the disciples. I was surprised by Jesus' strength and I said so.

They then read me another story where Jesus was at a house with a great crowd around him so there was no way to get near him. Then four friends brought a paralytic friend, and had to lower him through the roof just to get to Jesus. When Jesus saw their faith, he told the paralytic, "Your sins are forgiven." The Pharisees objected because they felt that no one can forgive sin except God. But Jesus showed them that he had authority to forgive sins.

This really made me think. Did Jesus truly have the authority to forgive sins as well as heal with just a word? I really loved hearing the stories of Jesus, this powerful, strange miracle worker.

This situation continued for a long time. Every day they would read me a few new stories of Jesus, and at the end of the week we would talk late into the night. Slowly I started to participate with them in their Christian prayers because they said it was not forbidden for me to do so. They said we were both praying to the same heavenly Lord, so there is nothing wrong with participating in their prayers. Yet, I continued to do my Islamic prayers and reading the Quran, and would only go to them after finishing all of my prayers.

This was the first time in my life to pray a completely different kind of prayer than my Islamic prayers, without ablution, and long clothes (though they did actually cover their hair during prayer like I was used to). I was beginning to feel happy but I didn't know exactly why. I felt that maybe I was seeking to be more near to God, because I had always had a feeling that something was missing in my worship, and the Christian prayers were completing what I felt was missing. I did my Muslim prayers and I prayed with my Christian friends, so I felt that with two kinds of prayers, maybe God was more pleased with me. I can truly say that my heart's desire was to please God and be near him even though I didn't know how.

More Christians become part of my life

During these same days, something else happened. In our village of Krimpen A/D Ijssel near Rotterdam, there were a lot of churches, and every Sunday I used to hear the church bells ringing in the morning. One of these churches had volunteers who helped the foreigners coming to their country.

Because The Netherland is a European country which supports and defends human rights regardless of religion, color, or sex, it opens its doors to serve the affected from the Third World countries, and gives them a chance to experience a new life, without imposing any religion on anyone.

The church volunteers were eager to bring the real light to the refugees. They behaved with humility, love, and patience as they did good works, and shared the gospel of Jesus Christ message with the lost. They used to come to the camp and knock on the doors and ask if they could do anything to help people with the difficulties they were facing in the language or with fitting into their society or learning the rules, regulations and culture of their country.

One day, a young woman knocked on my door and said, "I live nearby and came to see if there's anything I can do to help you in your new life in The Netherlands." This woman was a volunteer from one of the nearby churches that helped refugees, free of charge. I was surprised at her simple clothes, her smile, and the obvious love she had in her eyes, so I invited her to come into my room. She introduced herself to me and said, "If you ever need any kind of help, please call me," and then she left. After that I told the family that I lived with about her. They were surprised and told me that the Dutch people were so much different than we were. Then I started to hear from the other neighbors that I met in the laundry room or the kitchen that this same woman who visited me was a Christian Missionary who, under the excuse of helping people with the language, wanted to convert me.

I was told that she was not the only one, but there were others who came to our place. I was warned to be careful of opening the door to her or to any of these Dutch Missionaries, who work to attract others to their Christian religion.

I didn't take seriously the word of these people who were warning me. I wasn't the kind of person who just believed anything people told me. Even when I was a child, I was not easily convinced by words; I had to discover the truth by myself. So I said that I must open the door to these people and find out if what people said about them was true. Because I'm from an Arabic culture, I know very well how people exaggerate when they tell stories about others.

I also thought that this would be a great opportunity for me to talk to the Dutch people about Islam, about the Prophet Muhammad, and about the Quran. I could lead them to the truth, convert them to Islam, and by this way, I would gain huge benefits on this earth and in heaven. I could teach them to pray like I did and make my beloved father happy. He had a great desire to spread Islam to infidel countries, and gain big benefits in heaven.

After a while the same woman, whose name was Gerda, came back, even though I hadn't called her. She was very kind and tender and she got to know my friends, the Christian Iraqi family, and she started to help us with several things. She took time in her busy life to come and see what I needed and met my needs without me asking.

A gift of unconditional love

In The Netherlands it's a must to have a bicycle. We needed it to get around. I was in need of one but had no money to buy one. Gerda knew of my need and one cold and rainy evening at 9 pm, I was lying in bed cuddled in my heavy blanket when I was surprised by a knock on my door. It was Gerda! She said, "Come outside, I have a surprise for you!" I said surprisingly, "NOW? It's cold and raining outside!" She said, "Come outside quickly, don't be lazy." What an amazing surprise it was! A beautiful blue bicycle. She said it was mine!! I couldn't believe it! I hugged her and kissed her immediately. I got on the bicycle and rode it in the rain and cold in the yard of the camp. I didn't care about the cold or the rain. I was full of freshness, joy and warmth.

Gerda was watching me ride the bicycle with joy on my face, and she felt happy too because she had made me happy. She told me to take care of the bicycle and said good bye. She said she had to return quickly to her home. "But, how are you getting home?" I asked. Her answer shocked me. She had to walk back home because she had ridden the bicycle to give it to me. The walk home would take her over two hours! When she saw how worried I looked, she told me not to worry, that she would enjoy the evening exercise.

I couldn't believe this woman's love and generosity. I cried to think of her walking through the forest in the rain and cold in the harsh winter, only to help a complete stranger and make me happy. This situation affected me tremendously, and I will remember it always. I asked myself what could be the secret of this amazing and deep love? Why would she love me, a foreigner from the Middle East who had no relation to her?

The first conflict

Gerda invited me to the church that she worshipped at in a nearby small village named "Krimpen A/D Lek." She wanted to introduce me to the Dutch community. The pastor, Matthias, was a big hearted man who was very friendly. I also met another pastor from Pakistan whose name was Elijah, and a young lady whose name was Karolina. They were so happy when they heard that I was a Muslim and they didn't ask me anything about my religion. They only said to me that I should consider that I now have a family and friends in this country.

I was so delighted by their welcome. I used to imagine that western people were cold and didn't have feelings. When I was young they had taught us that western people didn't like foreigners. But I was so wrong. My new friends, Karolina and Elijah, came to visit me and I introduced them to the Iraqi family whom I lived with and prayed with every night. They prayed with us and invited us to their church, and we promised them that we would go the next Sunday.

Sunday came, and the pastor himself came to pick us up. I went with my Iraqi family friends. After the service started and they sang a few songs, Pastor Matthias said, "Today I'll speak in English because you can't understand the Dutch language yet. However, I understand that even English is hard for you to understand." So Pastor Matthias asked me if I was willing to translate for them. At first I refused because my English was so weak, as I hadn't studied English for a very long time. But I started to translate a little bit of what I heard, and the pastor was very encouraging. He said my translation was very good, and I was glad for the compliment.

I returned from church full of joy, I didn't know why. Maybe because I had a chance to stand in public and translate. Maybe because they encouraged me and I felt self-confident. I had never imagined that one day I would translate from English to Arabic. This was the last thing I could have expected in my life.

But that night my joy came to a dead end when a big problem happened with my aunt, the first of many problems with her. I was in the habit of visiting her on the weekends, but that week I didn't go, and I turned off my mobile phone during my time at church, so my aunt got worried and called me in the evening to find out what had happened to me, and why I had not gone to see her nor answered my phone that morning. Because I didn't know how to give an excuse for my visit to the church, I told her hesitantly and in a shaky voice that I was working. She, however, was full of doubt and wondered what kind of work I could be doing in a country where I didn't know the language. Also, she knew that there was no work on Saturdays and Sundays in The Netherlands. She demanded I tell her the truth of where I'd been.

I felt that her imagination was running away with her, so I said, "Please don't mistrust me, aunt. I was really working. I was translating in a church. They asked me to help them."

She shouted, "Church?!! Have you gone crazy to enter a church? You must refuse immediately." I said, "But I really enjoyed translating to improve my English language." She said, "If you like translating, there is a big opportunity here and lots of people who need help in this country. You're living in The Netherlands and don't need English at all, and should concentrate on studying the Dutch language only."

I replied that I didn't want to forget my English because it is a universal language. But she kept scolding and warning me never to enter a church. I kept reassuring her that I was a devoted Muslim and I would always adhere to the rules of Islam.

My introduction to Jesus' teaching

Two days later, Karolina and Elijah came to visit us again and see what we were needing the most. We said that our biggest problem was that we needed a new place to live. They sat down and prayed for us and their prayer was from the bottom of the heart. Their words were so beautiful and earnest. They encouraged us to come again to church on Sunday.

We went on Sunday, and Pastor Matthias invited me to translate. I tried but I felt so embarrassed because my translation of the Biblical words to Arabic was so weak, so I decided not to put myself in such an embarrassing situation again. I told Matthias that I was making lots of mistakes, though inside my heart I had a great desire to do this work. I said I wouldn't come to church next Sunday because my translation was useless. He disagreed and said my translation was good. So in order to help me feel more confident, he said he would give me his sermon text ahead of time. He told me to read the fifth chapter of Matthew several times and study it well so I could be ready for Sunday. He gave me a dictionary to help me with the translation, and told me to call him in case I faced any difficulty.

I went home and started to read the fifth chapter of Matthew. It was a life changing night. I read teachings and philosophies that night I had never imagined existed. I read it all in the same night and continued to read it again and again. I underlined the verses that affected me, and made me think. Here is an example of the kinds of reactions I had to these verses. I read these two verses:

> *You have heard that our ancestors were told, 'You must not murder. If you commit murder, you are subject to judgment.' But I say, if you are even angry with someone, you are subject to judgment!* (Matthew 5:21).

This verse amazed me! I felt confused and said, "God, why is it that we, in Islam, are allowed to get angry for a reason or without a reason, but the anger in Christianity is a big sin equal to murder?" I felt strength in the words, and went to read the Quran, my book that I loved.

> *Fighting has been enjoined upon you while it is hateful to you. But perhaps you hate a thing and it is good for you; and perhaps you love a thing and it is bad for you. And Allah Knows, while you know not* (Surat Al-Bakarah 216).

> *And fight in the cause of Allah and know that Allah is Hearing and Knowing* (Surat Al-Bakarah 244).

I meditated on these verses a long time, wondering why my book, the Quran, orders us to fight. I got back to the Quran and found more verses talking about murdering:

> *So let those fight in the cause of Allah who sell the life of this world for the Hereafter. And he who fights in the cause of Allah and is killed or achieves victory - We will bestow upon him a great reward* (Surat An-Nisa' 74).

> *Those who believe, fight in the cause of Allah, and those who disbelieve fight in the cause of taghut. So fight against the allies of Satan indeed, the plot of Satan has ever been weak* (Surat An-Nisa' 76).

53

So fight, {O Muhammad}, in the cause of Allah; you are not held responsible except for yourself. And encourage the believers "to join you" that perhaps Allah will restrain the {military} might of those who disbelieve. And Allah is greater in might and stronger in {exemplary} punishment (Surat An-Nisa' 84).

Fight those who do not believe in Allah or in the Last Day and who do not consider unlawful what Allah and His Messenger have made unlawful and who do not adopt the religion of truth from those who were given the Scripture – [fight] until they give the Jizyah (tax) willingly while they are humbled (Surat At-Tawba 29).

As I started reading the Bible and comparing it to the Quran, I got annoyed with myself. I should not be comparing anything with the Quran, because I believed it was the true book of God. I continued reading in the Bible the following verses:

You have heard the commandment that says, "You must not commit adultery." But I say, anyone who even looks at a woman with lust has already committed adultery with her in his heart. So if your eye—even your good eye—causes you to lust, gouge it out and throw it away. It is better for you to lose one part of your body than for your whole body to be thrown into hell (Matt. 5: 27 – 29).

I was amazed by this verse. The words were noble and dignified. This was my dream, that men would be highly ethical and respect women, and have no lust in their hearts. The verse said, "has already committed adultery with her in his heart," which means that sin starts in the heart. I said to myself, "Oh, if only the Muslims in Saudi Arabia, Iraq, Jordan, or even here in my camp can read this. I would love it if I could go out now to those

54

Muslim youths who are standing outside looking at the girls, and read them this beautiful verse in a loud voice! I know they would think that I'm coming from another planet or have lost my mind, because these verses have such a high level of ethics that no one can live up to."

I repeated this verse many times, because I used to suffer from men looking at me, especially since I never wore the head covering when I was in Iraq. I used to hear from my father that women are shameful, but in this verse Jesus said "anyone who even looks at a woman with lust," therefore, the lust comes from the heart of the man, not the woman. Jesus also confirms that it's better for the man to live without eyes than to live with impure eyes, and this is what displeased God. Wow, how wonderful was this lofty teaching! I couldn't help comparing it with verses in the Quran, and asking myself why such noble things were not written in the Quran.

God says:

> *And if you fear that you will not deal justly with the orphan girls, then marry those that please you or other women, two or three or four. But if you fear that you will not be just, then marry only one or those your right hand possesses. That is more suitable than you may not incline [to injustice]* (Surat An-Nisa 3).

Also, there is another verse:

> *And "inkahu" the unmarried among you and the righteous among your male slave and female slaves, if they should be poor, Allah will enrich them from His bounty, and Allah is all-Encompassing and Knowing* (Surat An-Nur 32).

And of His signs that He created for you from yourselves mates that you may find tranquility in them; and He placed between you affection and mercy. Indeed in that are signs for the people who give thought (Surat Ar-Rum 21).

He created you from one soul. Then He made from it its mate (Surat Az-Zumar 6).

I continued to feel annoyed with myself for comparing the Noble Quran with the Bible, and because of the doubts that started to dance in front of my eyes during my Bible study. The reason I kept searching the Quran was to find something to give me hope and joy in my religion. But instead I was annoyed and I didn't know why. The results were not pleasing my heart.

I was mesmerized by this Bible and continued to read more. I came to the following verses:

You have heard the law that says,"A man can divorce his wife by merely giving her a written notice of divorce." But I say that a man who divorces his wife, unless she has been unfaithful, causes her to commit adultery. And anyone who marries a divorced woman also commits adultery (Matt 5: 31, 32).

This verse made me feel afraid whereas, in the previous verses, I was flying happily in the clouds because of the high levels of ethics I was reading about. Now I started to be afraid when I began to realize that divorce must be forbidden in Christianity. I began to say to myself that Christianity was too hard, forcing a woman to stay with a man whatever his morals or behaviors were. Is it also required, then, for a Christian man to keep his wife even if she had a sickness or bad temper? What if she treated him badly, or was careless with her housework or with herself? Is it a holy marriage till the end of life?

My mind went immediately to the practices of our Islamic community where a Muslim man can freely divorce, and for any reason. For example: if he wants to punish his wife, or if she's a little careless with the housework, a man has the freedom to marry another woman. I started to think of the women I knew who had been treated so unjustly by their hard husbands because of sickness, carelessness, childlessness, or when they got old, or for losing their beauty and agility. Many Muslim men put away their wives when they get old and take young women in their place. Islam allows men to freely marry other women whether or not the old wife agrees.

I also was distressed to think of the weakness in the marriage relationships of Muslims in comparison to Christian marriages and could not help seeing mercy in Christianity, but only hardness in Islam. Even before, I used to criticize the Islamic men's behaviors towards their wives. They were not loyal, but hard hearted. I searched in my mind and couldn't find one single example that showed any sign of loyalty or dedication of one Muslim man who would stay with his sick or weary wife.

The wife was required to be obedient and wise in everything and couldn't oppose her husband in anything or else her fate would be divorce or separation from her husband. Moreover, the wife in our Arabic and Islamic communities had to be patient and endure her husband whether he was sick, or sterile, or mentally insane, or angry, or proud, or immoral in his conduct. She had to live with him in repression, injustice, and sadness, because the community had no mercy on her. So rarely had I seen a wife avenge her dignity and seek a divorce, though recently the situation has changed a little.

I don't know why I was insisting on comparing what I was reading in the Bible with the Quran, and making life more difficult for myself. But the words I was reading were so compelling and so strong that they were penetrating my heart, and turning it upside down. I found the following saying in the Quran about divorce:

> *Divorce is twice. Then, either keep [her] in an acceptable manner or release [her] with good treatment. And it is not lawful for you to take anything of what you have given them unless both fear that they will not be able to keep [within] the limits of Allah . But if you fear that they will not keep [within] the limits of Allah , then there is no blame upon either of them concerning that by which she ransoms herself. These are the limits of Allah , so do not transgress them. And whoever transgresses the limits of Allah - it is those who are the wrongdoers* (Surat Al-Baqarah 229).

> *And when you divorce women and they have fulfilled their term, do not prevent them from remarrying their [former] husbands if they agree among themselves on an acceptable basis. That is instructed to whoever of you believes in Allah and the Last Day. That is better for you and purer, and Allah knows and you know not* (Surat Al-Baqarah 232).

> *And if he has divorced her [for the third time], then she is not lawful to him afterward until [after] she marries a husband other than him. And if the latter husband divorces her [or dies], there is no blame upon the woman and her former husband for returning to each other if*

58

they think that they can keep [within] the limits of Allah . These are the limits of Allah , which He makes clear to a people who know (Surat Al-Baqarah 230).

The last verse was very annoying to me. I believed that any reasonable Muslim wouldn't accept it because it dishonored the dignity of the man. How could a man give the wife that he divorced to another man then take her back? But the Quran accepted this readily, whereas the Bible rejected this even in Old Testament times.

Suppose a man marries a woman but she does not please him. Having discovered something wrong with her, he writes a document of divorce, hands it to her, and sends her away from his house. When she leaves his house, she is free to marry another man. But if the second husband also turns against her, writes a document of divorce, hands it to her, and sends her away, or if he dies, the first husband may not marry her again, for she has been defiled. That would be detestable to the LORD. You must not bring guilt upon the land the LORD your God is giving you as a special possession (Deuteronomy 24: 1- 4).

I was so shook up by all I was reading and thinking that I started to talk to myself out loud. In my thoughts I kept going over things in my background, my family and friends. I thought about how a woman in Islam lives in an insecure situation and always in fear that her husband will marry another woman because he is obeying the Quran which permits the man only to seek entertainment from women created to serve him.

I found these comparisons that I was making very hard, and they caused my stomach to hurt from the stress of thinking bad things about the Islamic religion, the religion that I was raised in and was part of me, in spite of the existence of injustice and cruelty in some of it. And there was something inside me that made me want to cover the defects that I was finding. I was feeling like a mother who delivers a baby with defects and she doesn't want to let anybody know about those defects because the child is her son and a part of her heart. This was Islam for me. It was like a son to me, a son that I loved in spite of what I was discovering. Yes, I loved it because it was a part of me and I was a part of it. I didn't want anybody to know the things that I was discovering at this time, and I didn't want anybody to hear what I was saying in my heart because I loved my religion from the bottom of my heart. Mostly, I loved my family and my relatives and Islam was part of them.

I said to myself, "Let me finish the fifth chapter of Matthew instead of doing this exhausting thinking." I read the following verse:

> *You have also heard that our ancestors were told, "You must not break your vows; you must carry out the vows you make to the LORD." But I say, do not make any vows! Do not say, 'By heaven!' because heaven is God's throne. And do not say, 'By the earth!' because the earth is his footstool. And do not say, 'By Jerusalem!' for Jerusalem is the city of the great King. Do not even say, 'By my head!' for you can't turn one hair white or black. Just say a simple, 'Yes, I will,' or 'No, I won't.' Anything beyond this is from the evil one* (Matthew 5: 33 - 37).

I liked this verse very much, and found it very practical for daily life. It is good to be a person of your word and not use the name of God lightly. Of course, I couldn't help comparing again with what I know to be the practice of Muslims. In Islam, swearing is used a lot, even for small things. Every time they swear they insult the God of glory. Most Muslims swear to make others believe their words. And on certain occasions that oath is a lie to gain something or to be saved from an embarrassing situation. When that happens, the required atonement is to give some money to the poor or fast for three days. By this, the sin will be deleted as if it had never happened.

Most people believe that if someone talks without swearing, that means they are not telling the truth, because swearing gives more affirmation and believability to the words. So I went to search the Quran to see if swearing is taught in the Quran or not. I was surprised to see that although Jesus forbids any kind of swearing, in the Quran, there is a lot of it.

God swore by himself:

> *So by your Lord, We will surely gather them and the devils; then We will bring them to be present around Hell upon their knees* (Surat Maryam 68).

> *Those who disbelieve have claimed that they will never be resurrected. Say, Yes, by my Lord, you will surely be resurrected; then you will be surely be informed of what you did. And that, for Allah, is easy* (Surat At-Taghabun 7).

> *By Allah, We did certainly send [messengers] to nations before you, but Satan made their deeds attractive to them. And he is the disbelievers' ally today [as well], and they will have a painful punishment* (Surat An-Nahl 63).

61

God swore by times:

> **By time indeed, mankind is in loss** (Surat Al-'Asr 1, 2).

> **By the morning brightness, and [by] the night when it covers with darkness** (Surat Ad-Duhaa 1, 2).

> **By the dawn and [by] ten nights** (Surat Al-Fajr 1, 2).

God swore by things:

> **By the fig and the olive and [by] Mount Sinai** (Surat At-Tin 1, 2).

> **And by the frequented house** (Surat At-Tur 3).

God swore by angels:

> **By those (angels) who pull out (the souls of the disbelievers and the wicked) with great violence; By those (angels) who gently take out (the souls of the believers); And by those that swim along (i.e. angels or planets in their orbits, etc.); And by those that press forward as in a race (i.e. the angels or stars or the horses, etc.); And by those angels who arrange to do the Commands of their Lord** (Surat An-Nazi'at 1 – 5).

Also in Surat Al-Safat, Surat Al-Thariyat, and Al-Murasalat, God swore by celestial phenomena:

> **By the sun and its brightness, and [by] the moon when it follows it, by the star when it descends, by the sky, displaying the Zodiacal signs**

God swore by the prophet Muhammad:

> **Verily, by thy life (O Prophet), in their wild intoxication, they wander in distraction, to and fro** (Surat Al-Hijr 72).

I came to understand from these verses why we Muslims are always swearing in small things and big things. With almost every sentence, we say Wallah (by God's name), so that it becomes like a habit of talking, as if our words are not reliable in themselves without swearing by God. We also swear by many other things such as Al-Kaaba (the place of the Hajj pilgrimage in Saudi Arabia), the Quran, our eyes, our age, our life. We even swear by our relatives, for example: I swear by my mother to do this or that.

This comparing was getting me more and more upset, and I started to think I needed to stop reading the Bible immediately and apologize to the pastor. I would just tell him I cannot translate for the church because reading the Bible was making me compare with the Quran, which would cause me ptoblems. I was a Muslim and proud of my religion and I didn't want to diminish its value. However, I decided in my heart that I should at least finish this homework of translating this one passage and then I would inform them that I would not be able to continue translating for them. So I came now to the following verse:

> *You have heard the law that says the punishment must match the injury: "An eye for an eye, and a tooth for a tooth." But I say, do not resist an evil person! If someone slaps you on the right cheek, offer the other cheek also. If you are sued in court and your shirt is taken from you, give your coat, too. If a soldier demands that you carry his gear for a mile, carry it two miles. Give to those who ask, and don't turn away from those who want to borrow* (Matthew 5: 38 – 42).

This verse captivated me, and made me stop for a long time and ask many questions. How can a human being keep silent in the face of abuse and humiliation? I applied it to myself and asked, "If

I were some place and somebody slapped me on the face, would I have to turn the other side? What does this hard teaching mean?" Reading the teaching of Jesus is beautiful, because it lifts us to a higher morality, even to the summit. But I concluded it was only ink on paper, and it could never be accomplished by a human being.

Jesus' words are not easy though they are deep and full of wisdom. I knew they were very hard to apply. When I am faced with insults or mistreated or hurt, I feel much pain and my way of dealing with it is to remove that person from my life. I determine not to see that person anymore, or hear anything about them or even accept their apology if it happens. This is my stubborn personality and the way I protect myself from being hurt. I get broken-hearted and hurt easily. I can't handle any hurtful words, or disrespectful behavior or hypocrisy from anybody.

I think there are a lot of people who are like me. I know that a lot of Arab women are like me in these matters because we Arab women come from the same communities and learn our attitudes from each other. We also take offense easily and have a lot of strife with the people around us over little things and big things.

The idea of accepting abuse from someone and remaining silent about it was beyond my comprehension. Did Christ want us to be a weak people? Or did he want Christians to be miserable people? To be hit, humiliated, laughed at, and their clothes taken from them while they stood there silently, calmly without defending themselves? I didn't know why Christ would say such a thing! In order for someone to live according to this verse, they would have to be a superman or would have to have power come straight from God in heaven to help them apply these words!

I remembered these verses in the Quran:

> *And we ordained for them therein a life for a life, an eye for an eye, a nose for a nose, and ear for an ear, a tooth for a tooth, and for wounds is legal retribution. But whoever gives [up his right as] charity, it is an expiation for him. And whoever does not judge by what Allah has revealed — then it is those who are the wrongdoers* (Surat Al-Ma'idah 45).

> *… whoever has assaulted you, assault him in the same way that he has assaulted you* (Surat Al-Baqarah 194).

Oh my God, please have mercy on me and save me from these painful comparisons. I was being so conflicted through what I was reading, but I felt compelled to keep at it and finish this chapter. I could ask the pastor about these hard things later.

I continued reading in Matthew chapter five:

> *You have heard that it was said, "You shall love your neighbor and hate your enemy." But I say to you, love your enemies, bless those who curse you, do good to those who hate you, and pray for those who spitefully use you and persecute you, that you may be sons of your father in heaven* (Matthew 43 – 45).

I had a violent reaction to this verse. It was even harder than the previous verse! I could see what a clever artist Jesus Christ was, taking his ethics step by step from one challenging level to another. My mind was exploding with the question, "How? How, how, and a thousand hows! "

How can Jesus order us to love our enemies?!! Enemies are depraved, malicious, ruthless, unjust people. They are like predators who try to crush us, who use our failures to malign us and dig a hole for us to fall into. But you Jesus, the righteous one, are asking me… No, thank God, he's not asking *me*. I'm not a Christian and will never be one, so I don't have to do this impossible thing. Thank God you ask the *Christians* to love their enemies, and you want them to bless those who abuse them. As for me, how can I love someone who hates me, humiliates me, takes me to court? How can I bless someone who spreads evil gossip about me? How can I do good to a person who wishes me to fall or who is jealous of me, depraved and evil in their actions towards me? It would take more than a miracle to accomplish this.

Love, in my opinion, is a warm gentle feeling in the heart. And there are many degrees of love—the way I love my mother, father, sister, and brother, each differ. The love of friends is another kind. It makes sense to love people who help you, or do something good for you. Love has a give and take aspect to it. Our parents love us and meet our needs, so it's natural to love them back. This is what love meant to me. But this verse turned the notion of love upside down in my mind. On what basis can someone love an enemy? Is that even possible? I felt that I would have to search to find the source of this kind of love. I began to say in my heart that this is a hard religion with high-level ideals, and can't possibly apply to real human beings living in this world.

I found that the next passage in the same chapter made much more sense to me:

> *If you love only those who love you, what reward is there for that? Even corrupt tax collectors do that much. If you are kind only to your friends, how are you different from anyone else? Even pagans do that. But you are to be*

perfect, even as your Father in heaven is perfect (Matthew 5: 46 – 48).

These verses struck me as very full of compassion and humanity and tenderness. I wished that my beloved father could read them. My father was actually full of compassion and humanity to the poor and I remember that he always brought the poor and strangers with him to the mosque to feed them and take care of them. Did that mean my father knew the Lord Jesus? No, but in my heart I was sure that if he read what I was reading now, he would believe in Jesus. But I wasn't about to send him a Bible. I remember he used to tell me, "These poor Christians are going to hell if they don't believe in Islam." At that moment, I wanted him to hear these beautiful teachings of Jesus Christ.

I couldn't sleep that night. Christianity seemed to me so deep and profound that I couldn't imagine any nobler teachings. They really were divine teachings, the kind I had wished for and dreamed of all my life. On one level I wished to be a part of that depth of religion, but the reality was that I was a Muslim and I had to stick with my Islam however noble and beautiful the words of Jesus were. I can get to know them on the surface, but I must not forget that my highest goal was to spread the message of Islam to the Dutch community that was drowning in the darkness of infidelity, freedom, corruption, and Christianity.

I did not stop with chapter 5. I was very curious and read more later. The teachings of Jesus Christ in Matthew 6 about charity and prayer were deeply profound and impressive to me:

When you pray, don't be like the hypocrites who love to pray publicly on street corners and in the synagogues where everyone can see them. I tell you the truth, that is all the reward they will ever get. But when you pray, go away by yourself, shut the door behind you, and pray to your Father in private. Then your Father, who sees everything, will reward you. When you pray, don't babble on and on as people of other religions do. They think their prayers are answered merely by repeating their words again and again (Matthew 6: 5 – 7).

"This means that prayer should be in a closed room, alone and quiet," I thought, "The purpose is not to show others that I'm a religious person superior to those who don't pray." This was the first time that I had heard that prayer should be a solitary conversation between me and the God whom I worshipped. For me, when I prayed I usually forgot to think of God or talk to him. Prayer was like a homework that I had to complete so I could have a clear conscience that I had performed my duty and removed that responsibility from my shoulders.

Everything is different here. I found these verses were touching my heart and attracting me. They felt honest and true.

Jesus' approach to fasting was also different from the Muslim ways I grew up with. He said:

And when you fast, don't make it obvious, as the hypocrites do, for they try to look miserable and disheveled so people will admire them for their fasting. I tell you the truth, that is the only reward they will ever get. But when you fast, comb your hair and wash your face. Then no one will notice that you are fasting, except your Father, who knows what you do in private. And your Father, who sees everything, will reward you (Matthew 6: 16 – 18).

68

I liked this verse very much, especially the words "except your Father who knows what you do in private." It's clear that all worship is to God, whether you're a Christian or a Muslim. But, in the Bible, God is our spiritual Father. I thought of what being a father meant. It meant he was family, and if he was my father, then he loved me because fathers love their children. It meant that he saw me as his small daughter and he knew me and so he would accept my prayers even if they were imperfect. It meant also that he somehow lived with me in the house because fathers usually live with their children.

So, the God of Christianity is a father living with his children, but the God of Islam, whom I worshipped and prayed to, is so distant. I never knew who he was to me, and I never knew whether or not he loved me. In fact it was not important for him to love me. The only important thing was for me to obey his commands, especially to pray five times a day.

As for Jesus' words regarding fasting, they really made an important distinction from Islam. It's a very important issue for Muslims to let the others know that they are fasting, especially in the month of Ramadan. We earn respect by doing so. I always told myself that this month of fasting was a holy month full of blessings. I did not put on my regular makeup so people would know I was fasting. But in Christianity this verse was stressing that I should act normal as if I were not fasting at all. Nobody needs to know that I'm fasting, because fasting is for the Holy God only.

Next I read some verses showing the importance of the eye:

> **Your eye is a lamp that provides light for your body. When your eye is good, your whole body is filled with**

light. But when your eye is bad, your whole body is filled with darkness. And if the light you think you have is actually darkness, how deep that darkness is (Matthew 6:22 – 23).

What beautiful words! The good eye is the eye that looks in one direction at one target, to one God, one Lord. But the bad eye is the eye that looks in every direction except the direction of God. This direction is away from the light source that lights our eyes and our lives.

Jesus said that he is our light and the light of the world. He alone is the source of salvation and the giver of the light of life. I had never heard words like this before and I was now more disturbed and distressed than ever, but also somehow excited because religion was not as grim as it had always been.

2

Why Should I Accept Jesus?

I was living in conflicting worlds regarding my spiritual life. As a Muslim, I was still practicing my ritual prayers, and daily reading the Quran. In the evening, after my dinner time prayer and Quran reading, I was praying with my friends, the Iraqi family, who treated me like a daughter. I shared real love and respect with them and we were gathering to pray and read the Bible every evening while we lived in the refugee camp in Krimpen. And, I was going to church every Sunday to translate the Word of God from English to Arabic.

During that period there was an Iraqi man, named Martin, who was filled with the Holy Spirit and very zealous for the Word of God. He had a desire to gather the Arab Christians in The Netherlands for the first Arabic conference in the country. So he started calling churches and it happened that he contacted the church I was going to. He asked Pastor Matthias if he had any Arabs in the church. The pastor said that he did and that there was a sister from Iraq who was helping with translation, and also an Iraqi family that came regularly.

The pastor gave Martin my phone number. Soon afterwards, Martin called me, thinking I was a Christian, and started to speak to me in the Ashurian language which is used by Christians in Iraq. I said to him, "I don't speak the Ashurian language. I'm from Baghdad." He invited me to come to the Conference in Tilbourg City in the south of The Netherlands, and he asked me to invite the Iraqi family that I knew.

I didn't commit to going, but I went immediately to my beloved Iraqi family and told them, "I have good news for you. There's an Arabic conference and you're invited to it." When they heard that, they were excited because we didn't know any Arabs except those that were living in the same refugee camp. I gave them Martin's number so they could get more details about the conference. They said, "For sure we'll all go and you too will go with us." But I said, "Please leave me alone. I have enough problems with my aunt. Don't you remember how much trouble I got into when she first found out that I went to church? If she hears that I went to a Christian conference, there will be a much bigger problem. I don't want problems with my family!"

I was actually *afraid* of my aunt. She was like my mother, and she felt she had authority over me, forcing me to obey her commands because she thought that she was doing what was right for me. Also, as a dutiful Arab niece, I was obligated to obey her whether I wanted to or not. What she said about Christians was that they were weak and poor and we needed to lead them to Islam, so I felt I was required to do that.

Now, all the church members started trying to convince me to attend the conference. One dear sister who played the guitar at church promised that she would take me back home immediately if I felt unhappy or uncomfortable. The reason my Dutch Christian friends were insisting for me to go to the conference was that they cared about me and wanted me to hear the Word of God in my own language. So far, all I had heard from God's Word was in English or Dutch, and these two languages were not my mother tongue.

With all this encouragement and insisting, I agreed to go, but actually I was afraid and didn't want to go. I told myself that at the last minute, while they were in the car, I would apologize profusely and tell them that I was not comfortable and to please understand my situation.

The family started to pack their things for the trip. They were so excited! When the travel day came, I was totally packed and ready to go with them but my plan was to wait till we got into the car to back out. A mini bus that holds about 10 passengers came to pick us up. When I got into the bus, I couldn't open my mouth! I don't know what happened! Something closed my mouth and I couldn't reject their insisting.

Accepting Jesus Christ as my savior

We arrived at the conference grounds, to small cabins in a big forest. When we got there, I was suddenly scared by the new atmosphere, and I didn't want to have to answer any questions. I didn't want people to find out that I was a Muslim. I felt strange because I was a Muslim but admired Jesus and was attending a Christian Conference. I was also afraid to reveal my full name and have my cousins and my aunt find out. All my fears centered on my family finding out that I was at a Christian Conference and among Christians.

The first day passed quietly. I stayed with my friends, the Iraqi family, and everybody thought I was really their daughter. But on the second day, something happened that I hadn't counted on. The speaker was giving a message about salvation and talking about the power of Jesus' blood poured out for me to save me from sin and erase all my mistakes and failures. Jesus loved me perfectly and eternally, but his love was practical in that he gave himself on the cross to redeem me. Yes, Jesus redeemed me with his blood, and I was brought here to this place by a special invitation from him who wanted to enter into my life and heart and dwell with me.

The words were penetrating my heart like sharp arrows. I had been hearing much about Jesus for almost a year, but this day I got to know the truth about his death on the cross for me, and I started to shake from the intensity of emotion. My tears started to fall like rain. Suddenly I stood up in the middle of the congregation and started to cry with water pouring out of my eyes and nose. My face was so sweaty. I didn't know what was happening to me. After the service I went to the pastor who was eager to talk, having noticed my tears and emotions. He said immediately, "I want to pray with you, would you like to invite the Lord Jesus into your life and accept him as your Savior and Lord of your life?"

I immediately answered yes without fully understanding what he meant. I just knew that I wanted this loving God who loved me so absolutely and died for me personally on the cross, pouring out his blood for me. I wanted this person who guaranteed me eternal life. I wanted so much to have Jesus as Lord of my heart and to be related to this beloved Master and have his name engraved on my soul. I wanted this loving, tender, calm and strong shepherd to protect me from all enemies. I felt like I was falling in love with Jesus and suddenly I cried:

> "I love you, Lord! You are my strength! Jesus, you are my rock, my fortress, my savior, the God I take refuge in. Until now, I only knew *about* you, but now I know *you* and I finally can understand much more of what I've been hearing about you during this past year because now, you let me hear it in Arabic and truly understand it."

It was July 15th, 2002 at 7:10 PM. I will never ever forget that date when the love of Jesus entered my heart. I felt suddenly that he was my beloved who was incarnated to me by the beautiful words I heard, and that he was the one who first loved me and his love was surrounding me so that I could never leave him. I didn't want this lovely feeling to leave me for a second. It was such a strong love that took over my feelings.

I spent that day at the conference in great joy. I felt a big change in me. I didn't know what it was, but the change appeared on my face for everybody to see. I wished so much that he could appear to me so I could fall on my face before him and cover his feet with kisses. The joy that filled me was so strong, reaching a level that I can't explain in words, and I don't think there's a language that could express what I was feeling at that time.

On the last day of the conference, the pastor asked those who were touched by Jesus or who gave their lives for the first time to Jesus to please stand up and share. Actually the words were for me, but I didn't dare confess in front of the whole group because I was so shy and afraid. But the pastor singled me out, so I stood up, confounded, and said, "I thank the Lord Jesus because he touched my heart." Then I sat down quickly. My face was red with embarrassment. I didn't want to speak in front of people and I didn't want to expose my new relationship with Jesus. I was still afraid that my aunt would find out what had happened.

Of course on the last day of the conference, we were all sad because the beautiful time had ended quickly. I came to this place empty but now I knew the Lord Jesus and was filled with a new love that overwhelmed me. I also got to know a nice group of believers. I didn't understand at that time that the step I had taken at the conference would be the guiding light for all the rest of my life, and would change the entire direction of my life forever.

Living in two worlds

After the conference I felt an overwhelming happiness, a wide smile on my face all the time. My heart was full of unusual love for all the people who lived in my camp. I even began to see the annoying people differently. I began to take their annoying behaviors lightly. But the amazing thing is that even after the conference I didn't stop praying the Islamic prayers five times a day and reading the Quran.

I continued to go to church on Sundays to translate and participate in prayer with my friends and my Christian neighbors. Even though I was still reading the Quran, I had a strong desire to read the Bible. Each morning I would read one of the psalms and then read through the book of Matthew. I was eating up the words and delighting in the reading. This added more beauty and joy to my life, because I was learning something new every day. Martin, who invited me to the conference, started to come to the camp and teach me and the Iraqi family.

In spite of the fact that I had accepted the Lord Jesus, was steeped in a Christian atmosphere, reading the Bible, taking discipleship classes, and translating at church, I considered myself a first class Muslim. I just felt that I had something more: Jesus in my life. What a beautiful addition he made to the basics that I had! I never imagined or considered leaving the Islamic religion, the religion of my fathers and grandfathers, the one that I was raised in and taught to consider as the right religion, the last heavenly religion that all people must follow.

The second conflict: Who is greater, Jesus or Muhammad?

After the conference, I had to visit my aunt because it had been a long time since I had gone to see her. I truly loved my aunt (Um-Saad) from the bottom of my heart in spite of her external harshness. She was a loving, inwardly kind, and very welcoming person. However, now I had something boiling inside me. My heart had changed and I was in love with a master called Jesus. I didn't know how I was going to announce this to my aunt's family.

During that time, one of the believers had given me a taped message describing the life of a monk who had lived an ascetic life of prayer. It told about how one day, he was visiting a prison to talk to the criminals on death row. That day, while he was praying with them, one of the prisoners closed the door and trapped him inside the prison, saying:

> You come here every day to pray for us, but we only have a few days left to live and we need to know the answer to one question, "Who is the greater, Jesus or Muhammad?" We won't let you out of here until you answer us.

The monk was scared and started to pray:

> O Lord, lead me to what I can say, please lord help me and have mercy on me. If I say Muhammad is greater than Jesus, the Christians will kill me, and if I say Jesus is greater than Muhammad, the Muslims will kill me because they have nothing to lose. If they kill one more person it won't change their death sentence.

The Lord had mercy on the monk and inspired him to give them this answer:

> Listen all of you. I have some information about each of them. I will tell you and you judge for yourselves.

> Regarding their births, Jesus was born of a virgin who didn't know a man, which means Jesus was born by a miracle from a mother without a father, but Muhammad was born like other human beings from a mother and a father.

> Jesus performed countless miracles, healed lepers, gave sight to blind people, cast out demons that lived in people, raised up dead people and made them alive again. But we've never heard that Muhammad did any miracles.

Jesus had authority over Nature, walking on water, and calming storms with a Word. But Muhammad didn't have authority over Nature.

Jesus taught by parables and wise teachings, but Muhammad didn't teach with parables.

Jesus never killed anyone, but Muhammad killed many people and carried out many invasions.

Jesus knew what was going to happen before it happened, but Muhammad couldn't foretell the future.

Jesus spread his message in peace and love, and prevented his followers from using the sword, while Muhammad spread his message by the sword, and urged his followers to fight.

Jesus didn't marry but remained pure all his life, while Muhammad married many wives.

Jesus had power over Satan, and demons were afraid of him, but Satan had power over Muhammad.

Many prophecies were written about the coming of Christ hundreds of years before he came, and all were fulfilled. But we've never heard about any prophecy written about Muhammad.

Jesus died on the cross and came back to life after three days. His tomb is empty and he is still living now, but Muhammad was killed and buried in a tomb and has remained there.

This was the story told on the tape and I took this message with me to my aunt's house hoping to use it to introduce them to Jesus. So they began to listen to the tape, but when the monk started making his arguments, my aunt's husband stopped the recorder and said, "This is Christian propaganda aimed at insulting the Lord of creation and the last Prophet of God, Muhammad (God's praise and peace on him)." They refused to listen to the rest of the tape during my stay in their house, and they got very upset by the message and asked me why I brought it and what I wanted to know.

I said, "I heard this and it made me wonder, so I would like to know the truth from you." They said that I should not believe this sacrilege. They asked me why I was being attracted towards Christianity. From that time, doubts about me started to enter into my aunt's heart, and I didn't know what happened after I left their home. I don't know if they listened to the rest of the message or not.

A shock to my Muslim faith

Something happened one day that changed the direction of my life. The Iraqi family and I were like children growing every day in grace. Every night after dinner the family, whom I considered my real family, gathered to read out of the Old and New Testaments and to study out of The Life Application Bible that had some simple explanations.

Na'el, the father, had a book called Hywar Sarieh Howla el Islam (True Conversation about Islam) that spoke frankly about Islam. He read it and told his family about it and they were all shocked to hear the truth about the Prophet Muhammad's life. However, they were hesitant to tell me. Day after day they saw me participating with them in prayer and reading the Bible after finishing my Islamic prayers and reading the Quran. I was continuing in the same empty cycle, without any real change in my life though I had accepted the Lord Jesus as my Lord and Savior.

One night, Na'el told me, "You still pray the Islamic prayer and believe in Muhammad as a prophet, but he is not a real prophet. Did you know Khadijah, his first wife, was actually a Christian and Muhammad married her by a Christian marriage? And according to Christian standards, he couldn't marry another woman while she was alive. And did you know that her cousin Waraka Ibn Nofal who was a priest, was helping Muhammad with his message?"

These questions were like a blow to me. I didn't know what to say, but I opened my mouth and eyes, and Na'el told me that if I wanted to know the truth, I should read this book. His words seemed so accusing to me and my face showed it. But the family who always loved me told him to stop hurting me and causing me pain. They knew how sensitive I was and how much I loved my religion of Islam, even though I also loved Jesus and prayed to him.

I took the book and started reading. When I opened the first page, I read a clear attack against the Prophet Muhammad. I immediately asked for forgiveness from the mighty Allah. The writer was clearly an infidel. I couldn't continue reading and I angrily went back to their room and threw the book on the ground in front of them and said, "The person who wrote this book is a person who doesn't know ethics or propriety. How dare he write such things against the great Prophet Muhammad!" I greatly loved the Prophet though I didn't really know why. The Quran doesn't say that Muhammad loved me, or that he did something to prove his love for me, but to me and all Muslims there's a deep love for the Prophet. He's part of our hearts, and Muslims can't bear to hear anything bad spoken about him.

Now, even though I got upset by the book, and couldn't read it, I eventually took it and put it between my Dutch language books. A discussion about the book took place one evening while I was praying with my friends. They told me that the writer of the book was a Muslim and an Imam in a Mosque. He was faithful in his worship and, being alone in the world, he used to read the Quran constantly and teach it during Friday prayers. He was at that time blind to the reality of Islam.

This man took a pilgrimage to Al-Hajj to complete the rituals of Islam, and during his rounds around Mecca he saw Jesus saying to him:

> I'm the God that you must worship. You are wasting your time here walking around a rock. This is not my home and I don't live in a house made by human beings. I am Jesus. I'm the beginning and the end. I can give you salvation. I'm your Savior. I'm alive and I'm the judge. All who believe in me will have eternal life.

The man fell down on his knees and said, "My Lord and God!" He took off the white Hajj clothes and returned to the hotel. He immediately left Islam and returned to Egypt where he researched and studied and discovered the truth about Islam and the Prophet Muhammad. Now, when I heard that conversation about the writer of the book, I didn't believe it because any talk against the Prophet Muhammad made me uncomfortable. I didn't want to know this truth, and didn't want to read anything painful about him.

An interesting thing happened to me soon after this. One morning when I grabbed my school schedule quickly before going to school, that wretched book fell in front of me. I returned it to its place, but the next day the same thing happened again. I was surprised and said to myself angrily, "I don't want to read this book!" But when this happened the third time, I had the feeling that there was something I needed to know and that the book was inviting me to read it. So I decided to read this book though I was afraid of finding things in it that I wouldn't like and that would trouble my heart and baffle my life.

I closed the door, locked it, and started reading.

What I learned from the book—things I was not aware of regarding Islam and the Prophet Muhammad

Muhammad and the spiritual creature

Muhammad, born in 570 Ad (The Elephant Year), was the son of Abdullah Bin Abdul-Mutaleb the son of Hisham. When he was born, his father died and his mother gave him to a woman in the desert to feed him and to raise him. After a few years, his mother also died, so his grandfather took care of him until he was 8 years old. After his grandfather died, he lived with his uncle Abu-Talib, a very poor man.

When Muhammad was 25 years old, he started to work with the trade caravans for a rich forty year old woman named Khadijah Bint-Khuwailed who asked him to marry her. He and his uncle agreed because they were very poor and she was very rich.

When Muhammad was 40 years old, a spiritual creature started to appear to him and say to him, "I'm the Angel Gabriel, and God has appointed you to be his Prophet." At first, Muhammad doubted this and wondered if this spiritual creature was an angel or a devil. He began to feel fear—terrible horror with his body shaking and his color changing. He would tell Khadijah, "I'm afraid of the demon," but she would calm him and tell him that Satan could not reach him. (Al-Seerah Al Halabiya page 380; Quranic Phenomenon page 140; Muhammad, Life Of pages 148-149.)

This is what Muhammad said regarding the visitations of this creature, "Gabriel came to me in Hira Cave, and said, read, but I said to him, I can't read. Then Gabriel started throttling me until I thought I was going to die, but then he released me and repeated, 'Read!' I said again, 'I can't read,' so Gabriel attacked me and squeezed me until I was unable to continue and thought I was dying. Gabriel said a third time, 'Read in the name of God the creator!'"

After that Muhammad went to Khadijah and told her what happened. He was in terror, having a nervous tic, and foaming at the mouth because he thought that he had seen the devil. But Khadijah calmed him and said, "Come sit on my left side," and he did. "Do you see him now?" she asked. He answered, yes. She then had him sit on her right side, and asked him if he still saw him. He said yes again and she got frustrated and took off her face covering and exposed her leg while Muhammad was sitting on her leg. Now she asked him if he still saw the creature and he said, No. She said, "This proves that he's an angel and not the devil, because when I exposed my face and legs he was embarrassed and ran away. The devil would not run away."

Accordingly, every time the Quran came to Muhammad, he used to have fainting spells, chills, and sweat heavily, even on cold days. His eyes would glaze over and he would become like a drunk, and then develop a severe headache and nervous cramps and a feeling that death was looming.

Right away, I could not understand how this could come from the Angel of God! The Angel of God should bring peace, calmness, joy, and reassurance. When the angel Gabriel visited the Virgin Mary to foretell the birth of Christ, he said to her, "Peace to you," and she was filled with peace, faith, and joy with great awe, but there were no nervous cramps or headaches or heaviness or horror.

Now the main question was this: "Was that spiritual creature, who was appearing to Muhammad in the cave of Hira and throttling him, the angel Gabriel or was it a devil?" It became clear that it was Satan who was appearing to Muhammad as the angel Gabriel, and this was confirmed by the reputable Islamic expositors Al-Halabi in Al-Seerah Al-Halabiya Part 1 page 163 and Al-Bukhari in Sahih Al-Bukhari Part 2 page 60.

Muhammad and his wives

I had previously heard, when I was in high school, that the Prophet had married a large number of wives in order to strengthen Islam and the relationships between Muslims as well as to increase the Muslim population by alliances with new tribes. But what I read in this book and what I found out when I did research afterwards, showed that none of the marriages was for the benefit of Islam, but for his own personal benefit only. I will explain this briefly.

There were 23 marriage contracts in the Prophet's life, but he entered into 12 of them only, and when he died, he had nine wives. Regarding the maids with whom the Prophet had sex, there were four according to Al-Seerah Al-Halabiya Book 3 page 417.

Khadijah Bint-Khuwailed was Muhammad's first wife, the cousin of the priest Waraka Bin-Nufal. She was married twice before him, and was 15 years older than him. He was 25 years old at the time of their marriage. Most opinions say that the priest Waraka, and therefore Khadijah, belonged to the Nasranyah group, a "Christian" group. Khadijah sued to marry Muhammad because she was rich and had influence on him since he was working for her. Research indicates that Muhammad married her according to her religious ways and with the blessings of Waraka the priest. Muhammad was faithful to this marriage and complied with the marriage terms during the whole time he spent with Khadijah. In other words, he did not marry anyone else until she died. He respected and loved her because he found in her the motherly tenderness that he lost when he was a child.

Aisha, Muhammad's second wife was 6 years old when he became engaged to her and he took her to wife when she was 9 years old and he was 51 (Al-Seyar Wal-Maghazi page 255; Biography of the Prophet Part 4 page 66; Sahih Al-Bukhari Part 5 page 71 and Part 7 pages 6 – 8; Sahih Muslim Part 3 page 578 – 579; History of Tabari Part 2 page 212). Muhammad had known Aisha since she was a baby and had seen her grow up. She was the most beloved of his wives. She is quoted describing her wedding day, "My mother came to me while I was on the swing. She took me down and combed my hair, then washed my face with water, and led me in. I entered and saw the Prophet of Allah sitting on the bed at our house. She put me in his lap and said, 'This is your wife —your family- God bless you in her,' then everybody left the house, and then the Prophet of Allah entered me. I was nine years old that day (Nisaa Al-Nabi, page 88).

The above mentioned Islamic references state that when Aisha went to her husband Muhammad's house, she brought toys with her as she was just a child. Even in those ancient days, it was not normal for an old man to marry a young child. Abu Baker, her father, was surprised and unhappy with the arrangement but consented under the pressure of Muhammad insisting. When the Prophet died, Aisha was 18 years old and became a very young widow and was forbidden to marry again.

Sawdah Bint Zamaa was an old widow, not beautiful, but she had a good heart and decent manners. Muhammad wanted to divorce her, but she begged him and gave her night to Aisha. Many can witness to this (Nisaa Al-Nabi pages 66 – 67).

Hafsa Bint-Omar was the fourth wife whom he married in Al-Medina after her husband, Khanees Fin-Huthafah Ah-Sahmik, died. She was a 20 years old immigrant, to whom Muhammad was attracted. Her father, Omar Bin Al-Khatab, was very happy about the marriage.

Zaynab Bint-Jahsh was the wife of Zayd Bin Haritha who had been kidnapped from the Bedouins and sold to Khadijah, Muhammad's first wife. She had presented him as a servant to Muhammad. Muhammad later gave Zayd his freedom and adopted him by saying, "Zayd is my son and heir and I name him Zayd Bin (the son of) Muhammad." Then, Muhammad asked his cousin Zaynab to marry Zayd but she refused because she felt he was below her status as she was the Prophet's cousin.

Muhammad then insisted on the marriage and said that a message had come to him from heaven saying to her and to all Muslims:

> *A faithful man or woman may not, when Allah and His Apostle have decided on a matter, have any option in their matter, and whoever disobeys Allah and His Apostle has certainly strayed into manifest error* (Surat Al-'Ahzab 36).

So Zaynab obeyed Allah and his Messenger Muhammad and went through with the marriage.

One day, Muhammad went to visit the couple, but Zayd was not home. Zaynab came out to welcome Muhammad before she had finished covering up in her clothes. Muhammad was attracted to her and went out saying, "Glory to the heart changer." It seems, by default, Allah always supports what Muhammad wants.

> *When you said to him whom Allah had blessed, and whom you [too] had blessed, "Retain your wife for yourself, and be wary of Allah," and you had hidden in your heart what Allah was to divulge, and you feared the people though Allah is worthier that you should fear Him, so when Zayd had got through with her, We wedded her to you, so that there may be no blame on the faithful in respect of the wives of their adopted sons, when the latter have got through with them, and Allah's command is bound to be fulfilled* (Surat Al-'Ahzab 37).

How can a Holy God ordain Zaynab to marry Zayd then cancel the same thing? Doesn't this make God out to be unfair? Would God be pleased for his Prophet to be attracted to a married woman? A true prophet should behave in a holy manner, rejecting immoral passions and controlling his lusts. We should expect Muhammad, if he is truly a prophet from God to ask God's help to maintain a pure heart and behave in a noble manner towards a married woman, especially when she's his adopted son's wife. One of Muhammad's wives is quoted as saying, "I can see Allah hurries to meet your desires, O Muhammad" (Sahih Al-Bukhari Part 7 page 16).

Safya Bint-Huye. In the seventh year of the immigration from Medina to Mecca, Muhammad defeated the Jewish tribe Khybe, killing many people, looting their property, and capturing their women. Safya was one of the prisoners. Muhammad ordered her father killed and tortured her husband Kinana Bin Rabee to get him to reveal the place his money was hidden. Once the man revealed the information, Muhammad, being 60 years old at the time, killed him and married his wife who was only 17 years old! It seems very cruel to kill a man, take his money and then marry his wife. Safya was not as young as Aisha, but the difference in age between her and Muhammad was 43 years (Al-Seerah Al-Halabiya Part 3 page 179; Sahih Al-Bukhari Part 1 Page 104 and Part 5 page 168).

Jouryah Bint Al-Harith was the next wife. Aisha is quoted to have said about her, "When Allah's Prophet divided the spoil of the conquered people of Bani Al-Mutliq tribe, Jouryah was selected in the division to be given to Thabit Ibn Qais. She was 20 years old and so beautiful that anyone who saw her was smitten to the core. By Allah, I saw her in front of my door and I hated her, because I was certain that the Prophet would see in her the beauty I saw."

Actually, Aisha was correct in her fears. When Muhammad saw Jouryah, he asked her to marry him and she accepted. After paying Thabit some money for her, Muhammad married her (Biography of the Prophet Part 3 page 157; Al-Seerah Al-Halabiya Part 2 page 586).

Um-Salama Al-Makhzoumyah was the sixth wife, a very beautiful woman. Aisha commented about her, "When the Prophet of Allah married Um-Salama, I was sad to hear so much spoken about her beauty, but when I saw her, I saw that she was even more beautiful than they described." When Muhammad first saw her at the house of Uthman Bin Afan, he inquired about her. Uthman replied that she was his sister's daughter and was married to Ghassan Bin Al-Mugherah. Twenty four hours later, Muhammad ordered her husband to be the flag bearer in the next war. The husband died in the war, and Muhammad married her the next day without regard for her feelings about her husband's death. He did not wait the required mourning period that she must observe before getting remarried. He had little regard for Aisha's feelings who describes herself as the closest to him, yet he was marrying a new woman every day, hurting her feelings and making her live in pain and sadness. He had more interest in satisfying his desires than for the feelings of those he loved.

Um-Habibah was another 23 year old beautiful wife. Muhammad married her after her husband Ubaid-Allah Bin Jahsh (Muhammad's cousin, and Zaynab's Brother) left Islam, immigrated to Ethiopia and became a Christian. This man was moved by the lives of the Christians in Habasha, believed in Christ, and was baptized. When this happened, Muhammad married Um-Habibah. Some Islamic references state that Muhammad was married twice in one week.

The Coptic beauty Marya was one of the Prophet's concubines, gifted to him by the Egyptian Governor. A story is told of her coming to visit Muhammad at Hafsa's house for the purpose of consulting him about a matter. Hafsa was not in the house and Muhammad was alone with her. Suddenly Hafsa came home and cried out, "I saw what you did, O Muhammad, in my house and on my bed and on my day." So Muhammad asked her to keep it a secret from Aisha, and promised to send Marya away. But Hafsa told Aisha, so the Prophet divorced Hafsa, though he took her back a while later.

He went ahead and married Marya Al-Coptiyya after Surat Al-Tahreem was given to him. Verse 1 states, *"O Prophet, why do you prohibit [yourself from] what Allah has made lawful for you, seeking the approval of your wives? And Allah is Forgiving and Merciful."* The news spread everywhere, and all of his wives boycotted him. There are a lot of Islamic references describing this incident (Al-Seerah Al-Halabiya Part 3 page 403; Nisa Al-Nabi starting from page 122; Unmasking Muhamad's Life; Al Baydawi explanation and Al-Jalalayn explanation page 64).

Maymouna Bint Al-Hareth The Prophet Muhammad forbade Muslims from marrying during the period of the Hajj. This is clear in Surat Al-Baqarah 1:9:

> *Hajj (pilgrimage) is [during] well-known months, so whoever has made Hajj obligatory upon himself therein [by entering the state of ihram], there is [to be for him] no sexual relations and no disobedience and no disputing during Hajj. And whatever good you do – Allah knows it. And take provisions, but indeed, the best provision is fear of Allah. And fear Me, O you of understanding.*

91

However, for himself, Muhammad made an exception and married Maymouna during that time (Sahih Al-Bukhari Part 3 page 18 and Biography of the Prophet Part 3 page 202).

I was deeply surprised, affected and disturbed by what I read about the Prophet Muhammad's biography. I was shocked and wanted to scream out loud, "How? How could this happen? Why didn't I know about his history before? Why didn't my father tell me about Muhammad's marriages? Maybe my father was afraid it would shock me. Or maybe he wanted to avoid the scandals! Or maybe he didn't know about all these matters." But how would my father not know these stories when they are all written in the Islamic references? Why did the Prophet devote himself to evil lust instead of solving the problems of his people and his nation? Isn't a religious leader supposed to devote himself to his flock and his people, and help them live in peace? Where could he even find time to think of his people when he had all these women?

I know that, in real life, a person in a leadership position can barely concentrate on his job, when he has just one wife and family. What I concluded from these stories, which were confirmed by Islamic references, was that the Prophet Muhammad loved himself and was mostly concerned about fulfilling his fleshly desires, without regard to the pain he caused others. I had hundreds of questions turning in my head, and felt so sad that the leader I was following had a life I would be ashamed of. I also concluded that it must be impossible that he was innocent when all of these Islamic references confirm the stories.

Muhammad's violence

I had learned much when I was young, in my history classes, but I had forgotten that Islam had been spread by the sword. Islam does actually say something about peace and freedom. For example, Surat Al-Baqarah 256 says:

> **There shall be no compulsion in [acceptance of] the religion. The right course has become clear from the wrong.**

In Surat Al-Kafirun, we read:

> **You have your religion and I have a religion.**

Muhammad started off by making peace with all the tribes around him. He did this first of all because he was weak militarily and financially in the early stage of his message. Secondly, he thought that peace was the best method to encourage Jews and Christians (Nasarah) to convert to Islam, but he discovered later that this peaceful approach did not help him to spread his message. He then got rid of the Jews in Al-Medina, formed an army of ten thousand warriors, and became a thriving influence in the Arabian Peninsula. In January of the year 630, Mecca surrendered to him after a difficult military siege.

Soon after that, the war and killing spread rapidly from Mecca and Medina to all over the Arab world, and then to Europe, North Africa and other places around the world.

I wanted to think that maybe the Prophet loved peace along with loving all those women, that maybe he was actually merciful and kind. But I was appalled to read about all the merciless killing he perpetuated. There's a famous incident that most Muslims don't know about, where Muhammad killed 800 - 900 men from the

93

Jewish Tribe Quraizah in the Bani Quraizah Foray. The Prophet waged this foray in the fifth year after migrating from Mecca to Medina. The important point is that the killing was not on the battlefield or during the war but after the tribe had surrendered and released their weapons to him. He consulted his advisors on what to do with them and decided to slaughter them all in one day. (You'll find the details in the following references: Muhammad, Life Of pages 347 – 351; Biography of a Prophet Part 3 pages 118 – 143; Al-Seerah Al-Halabiya Part 2 pages 657 – 677).

And I read another story that is so hard to accept about when the so called Prophet of Mercy killed an old woman named "Fatima Bint Rabeea." She was known as a courageous woman, but because she insulted Muhammad, he killed her in a horrible way. He tied each of her legs to a camel, and made them run so as to divide her into two halves. She had asked for pardon from Muhammad who refused and said, "For Allah, you will not even enter hell." This famous incident is recorded in all Muhammad's biographies by authors like Ibn Al-Atheer and Burhan Al-Deen Al-Halabi.

This reading was making me sick inside. Yet, in spite of what I read, and in spite of it all being supported in the Islamic references used by senior Muslim scholars in the Islamic universities, I could not give up on my religion. "But the Prophet Muhammad is after all a human being," I said inside my heart, still wanting to defend him.

What about the Noble Quran?

The next part of the book was about the Quran. So, before I started reading that part, I knelt and prayed, "O Lord, have mercy on me because the Quran is the most important thing in my life, and I know that the Quran is the miracle of Muhammad, and reading every single word and letter brings with it many blessings, as my father used to tell me."

The Quran actually quotes much of its information and stories from the Holy Bible, but with some additions or deletions. The Holy Bible is the original document written 600 years before the Quran. Additionally, there are verses that used to descend on Muhammad telling him to marry this woman or divorce that woman, etc. This Quran, according to the knowledge of Muslims, is a divine book. But how can it be divine and so full of language, historical, and scientific errors? It has instances where a verse would descend on the Prophet and then another verse would descend later to nullify it or contradict it.

Linguistic errors

Islam teaches that every word in the Quran came from God himself and therefore it has no mistakes. However there are many errors and inconsistencies in the text of the Quran. Some of these include the following:

> *[You disbelievers are] like those before you; they were stronger than you in power and more abundant in wealth and children. They enjoyed their portion [of worldly enjoyment], and you have enjoyed your portion as those before you enjoyed their portion, and you have engaged [in vanities] like that in which <u>he</u> engaged. [It is] those whose deeds have become worthless in this world and in*

the Hereafter, and it is they who are the losers (Surat At-Tawbah 69).

The underlined word should be "they," not "he," as can be seen in the context.

But those firm in knowledge among them and the believers believe in what has been revealed to you, [O Muhammad], and what was revealed before you. And the <u>establishers</u> of prayer [especially] and the givers of zakah (charity) and the believers in Allah and the Last Day – those We will give a great reward (Surat An-Nisa' 162).

In the Arabic version of the Quran, the word underlined above is not grammatically correct.

Other clear grammatical errors are found in Surat Al-Haj 19 and Surat Taha 63:

These two rivals fought.

These are two magicians.

In Arabic, there is a special verb form for the number two and these verse uses the wrong verb tense—an unacceptable mistake in Arabic.

The same mistake occurs in Surat Al-Maedah 69, Surat Al-Bakarah 124, Surat Al-Aaraf 56.

Contradictions in the Quran:

There are a lot of verses in the Quran that have clear contradictions, and Muslims don't know which of them to believe. For example, in Surat Al-Baqarah 256:

> *There shall be no compulsion in [acceptance of] the religion. The right course has become clear from the wrong. So whoever disbelieves in Taghut (Satan) and believes in Allah has grasped the most trustworthy handhold with no break in it. And Allah is Hearing and Knowing.*

This verse in the Quran affirms that everybody has the freedom to select his own religion, meaning everybody has the right to select a religion other than Islam.

But there are many other verses that state the opposite, as in Surat At-Tawbah 29:

> *Fight those who do not believe in Allah or in the Last Day and who do not consider unlawful what Allah and His Messenger have made unlawful and who do not adopt the religion of truth [Islam] from those who were given the Scripture – [fight] until they give the jizyah [tax] willingly while they are humbled.*

Surat At-Tawbah 73:

> *O Prophet, fight against the disbelievers and the hypocrites and be harsh upon them. And their refuge is Hell, and wretched is the destination.*

Surat An-Nisa' 89:

> *They wish you would disbelieve as they disbelieved so you would be alike. So do not take from among them allies until they emigrate for the cause of Allah. But if they turn away, then seize them and kill them wherever you find them and take not from among them any ally or helper.*

More examples are given in Surat Ar-Ra'd 40, and Surat Ash-Shuraa 8.

Here is another contradiction in Surat As-Sajdah 4:

> *It is Allah who created the heavens and the earth and whatever is between them in six days; then He established Himself about the Throne. You have not besides Him any protector or any intercessor; so will you not be reminded?*

This verse contradicts verses 9 – 12 in Surat Fussilat, which say that the earth was created in eight days.

Another contradiction is found in Surat Al-'A'raf 28:

> *And when they commit an immorality, they say, "We found our fathers doing it, and Allah has ordered us to do it." Say, "Indeed, Allah does not order immorality. Do you say about Allah that which you do not know?*

The contradicting verse is in Surat Al-'Isra' 16:

> *And when We intend to destroy a city, We command its affluent but they defiantly disobey therein; so the world comes into effect it, and We destroy it with [complete] destruction.*

This means they cause the rich to perform immoral acts so they can follow God's direction to destroy them for doing so.

The most important contradiction in the Quran, however, is about the death of Christ. In Surat An-Nisa' 157, we read:

> *And [for] their saying, "Indeed, we have killed the Messiah, Jesus, the son of Mary, the messenger of Allah." And they did not kill him, nor did they crucify him; but*

[another] was made to resemble him to them. And indeed, those who differ over it are in doubt about it. They have no knowledge of it except the following of assumption. And they did not kill him, for certain.

This contradicts verse 55 of Surat 'Al 'Imran:

[Remember] when Allah said, "O Jesus, indeed I will take you and raise you to Myself and purify you from those who disbelieve and make those who follow you [in submission to Allah alone] superior to those who disbelieve until the Day of Resurrection. Then to Me is your return, and I will judge between you concerning that in which you used to differ."

This translation in English is incomplete. In Arabic the term "I will take you and raise you" means "I will take you after I let you die."

In the last verse, the Quran confirms that Jesus died and that those who follow him are above others until the Last Day, not until the coming of the Quran.

Surat Maryam 33, also confirms the death and resurrection of Jesus:

And peace is on me the day I was born and the day I will die and the day I am raised alive.

Does God contradict Himself?

Many of the stories in the Quran that are taken from the Holy Bible contradict the Biblical narratives.

For example, regarding **Noah and the ark**, the Quran says in Surat Hud 42 and 43, that one of Noah's sons refused to enter the ark and drowned in the flood, while the Bible states that all three sons of Noah entered into the ark and were saved from the flood (Genesis 7:7).

Though **Abraham** plays an important part in the Quran, the facts about him have been changed. The Quran says that Abraham had two wives and two sons, while the Bible says he had three wives and eight sons (Genesis 25:1).

The Quran says that some of the descendants of Abraham lived in the Mecca Valley (Surat 'Ibrahim 37) while the Holy Bible says that they lived in Hebron (Genesis 13:18).

The Muslims mistakenly think that Abraham's son Ismael was the one who was selected to be sacrificed, even though the Quran doesn't mention the name, Ismael, at all:

> *So we gave him good tidings of a forbearing boy. And when he reached with him [the age of] exertion, he said, "O my son, indeed I have seen in a dream that I [must] sacrifice you, so see what you think."*
>
> *He said, "O my father, do as you are commanded. You will find me, if Allah wills, of the steadfast"* (Surat Al-Saffat 101 – 102).

The real story in the Holy Bible is clear that *Isaac* is the one who was to be sacrificed.

> *After these things God tested Abraham and said to him, "Abraham!"*
>
> *And he said, "Here I am."*
>
> *He said, "Take your son, your only son Isaac, whom you love, and go to the land of Moriah, and offer him there as*

a burnt offering on one of the mountains of which I shall tell you" (Genesis 22: 1 – 2).

The Quran says that Abraham built the Kaaba (Surat Al-Baqarah 125 – 127), while the Kaaba is not mentioned in the Bible and history tells us that it was built around the year 300 Ad.

With respect to **Moses**, the Quran says that Moses was adopted by Pharaoh's wife (Surat Al-Qasas 9) instead of his daughter as stated in the Bible (Genesis 5:2).

The Quran says that **Haman** lived in Egypt during the time of Moses (Surat Al-Qasas 6) while the Holy Bible says that he lived in Persia during the time of King Ahasuerus (Esther 3:1), which is about 1000 years after Moses.

The Quran also contradicts many facts about **Mary, mother of Jesus**. For example, the Quran says that Aaron was the brother of Mary (Surat Maryam 28) while the Holy Bible says that Aaron lived 1300 years before Mary (Numbers 26:59).

The Quran says that Mary delivered Jesus under a palm tree (Surat Maryam 23) while the Bible says that he was born in a manger (Luke 2:7).

The Quran says that **Essa** (another name for Jesus Christ in Arabic) talked in the cradle and performed miracles while he was a small child (Surat Maryam, 29 - 33) while the Holy Bible doesn't mention any of this.

The Quran says that **Zechariah** the father of Yehya was mute for three nights (Surat Maryam 10) while the Holy Bible says that he, Zechariah the father of John the Baptist, was made mute for nine months, until his son John was born (Luke 1:20).

After reading all this information that I didn't know before, and most Muslims don't know, I felt exhausted and fatigued. My mind could barely function any more. What next? All the tenets and basics of Islam had been destroyed right in front of me.

I could see from all this, however, and from my later studies, that the conditions that must be met in order for a man to be a prophet of God were not met by the Prophet of Islam, Muhammad.

1. A prophet must receive his call and message from God Himself. All the prophets in the Bible, including Moses, heard directly from God, whereas Muhammad never once heard from God but only from a creature that he himself first described as a devil to his wife Khadijah. To quote directly from Al-Seerah Al-Halabiya Part 1 page 337, Muhammad says, "I'm afraid that the one calling me is one of the demons... and I'm afraid that I'm crazy."

2. A prophet predicts something about the future. Muhammad, however, never had any predictions about the future, and said so about himself in Surat Al-'An'am 50:

> *Say, [O Muhammad], "I do not tell you that I have the depositories [containing the provision] of Allah or that I know the unseen, nor do I tell you that I am an angel. I only follow what is revealed to me." Say, "Is the blind equivalent to the seeing? Then will you not give thought?"*

3. Some prophets performed miracles, but the Prophet Muhammad never did. He never healed one sick person, or gave

sight to the blind, or exercised authority over diseases, nature, or demons. He was an average person with morals that are sometimes worse than the average person who protects women and behaves with integrity.

Muslims say that the Quran is the Miracle of Muhammad, but I say to them, "Where is the miracle? From what I read, the Quran has an endless list of language, grammatical, scientific, historical and geographical errors. These errors were made by the writer of the Quran."

4.   The character of a prophet should be above reproach.   A prophet of God must not be unjust or a murderer, but Muhammad was often unjust and killed a lot of innocent men, took their wives captive, and sold their children to buy weapons (Sunan Al-Kubra Part 9 page 129).

In the matter of holiness, unfortunately the Prophet Muhammad was not a role model, but he was a womanizer as verified over and over in the Islamic books that were written by well-known Islamic scholars who studied in Islamic universities.   (See the biographical books written about the prophet: Al-Tabaqat Al-Kubra, Part 1, page 398; Al-Seerah Al-Halabiya Part 3, page 377.)

In addition, lying does not demonstrate holiness, yet there are many common Islamic principles that allow for a Muslim to lie. For example:

War is a trick.

Necessity permits deceit.

If faced with two evils, choose the lesser one.

These principles are quoted from the Quran and Hadith (which is the record of what the Prophet Muhammad spoke).

Here are quotes from the Quran in which God sometimes permits Muslims to lie:

> *Allah will not impose blame upon you for what is meaningless in your oaths, but He will impose blame upon you for [breaking] what you intended of oaths. So its expiation is the feeding of ten needy people from the average of that which you feed your [own] families or clothing them or the freeing of a slave. But whoever cannot find [or afford it] – then a fast of three days [is required]. That is the expiation for oaths when you have sworn. But guard your oaths. Thus does Allah make clear to you His verses that you may be grateful* (Surat Al-Ma'idah 89).

> *Allah does not impose blame upon you for what is unintentional in your oaths, but He imposes blame upon you for what our hearts have earned. And Allah is Forgiving and Forbearing* (Surat Al-Baqarah 225).

> *Whoever disbelieves in Allah after his belief—except for one who is forced [to renounce his religion] while his heart is secure in faith—but those who [willingly] open their breasts to disbelief, upon them is wrath from Allah, and for them is a great punishment* (Surat An-Nahl 106).

In other words, Allah forgives Muslims' intentional lies by giving them acts of penance to do. The Muslim is allowed to swear and deny his faith in Allah if he is saying this without believing it.

The Islamic scholar Sheikh Al-Tabari (in History of Tabari) said, in his explanation of Surat An-Nahl 106, that this verse descended on Muhammad after he heard that Amar Bin Yasir was forced to denounce Muhammad when he was taken by the Bani Mugheerah Tribe. So after that happened, Muhammad said to him, "If they return, you can return." In other words, if they take you again, you can lie again.

5. The message of a true prophet should be a message of love, peace, and salvation. But actually Muhammad's message was quite the opposite and taught Muslims to be arrogant, proud and violent.

A prophet works for peace, but Muhammad was a man of war, who led 84 forays in 10 years while he was in Al-Medina. These forays were full of bloodshed, followed by plundering and looting.

The word "kill" is mentioned more than 100 times in the Quran, and below are some of the verses that require killing people who are not Muslims:

> *And kill them wherever you overtake them and expel them from wherever they have expelled you, and fitnah (persecution and injustice) is worse than killing. And do not fight them at al-Masjid al- Haram until they fight you there. But if they fight you, then kill them. Such is the recompense of the disbelievers* (Surat Al-Baqarah 191).

> *Fight them until there is no [more] fitnah (persecution and injustice) and [until] worship is [acknowledged to be] for Allah. But if they cease, then there is to be no aggression except against the oppressors* (Surat Al-Baqarah 193).

> *Fighting has been enjoined upon you while it is hateful to you. But perhaps you hate a thing and it is good for you;*

and perhaps you love a thing and it is bad for you. And Allah Knows, while you know not (Surat Al-Baqarah 216).

They ask you about the sacred month - about fighting therein. Say, "Fighting therein is great [sin], but averting [people] from the way of Allah and disbelief in Him and [preventing access to] al-Masjid al-Haram and the expulsion of its people therefrom are greater [evil] in the sight of Allah. And fitnah (persecution and injustice) is greater than killing." And they will continue to fight you until they turn you back from your religion if they are able. And whoever of you reverts from his religion [to disbelief] and dies while he is a disbeliever - for those, their deeds have become worthless in this world and the Hereafter, and those are the companions of the Fire, they will abide therein eternally (Surat Al-Baqarah 217).

And fight in the cause of Allah and know that Allah is Hearing and Knowing (Surat Al-Baqarah 244).

So let those fight in the cause of Allah who sell the life of this world for the Hereafter. And he who fights in the cause of Allah and is killed or achieves victory - We will bestow upon him a great reward (Surat An-Nisa' 74).

Those who believe fight in the cause of Allah, and those who disbelieve fight in the cause of Taghut (Satan). So fight against the allies of Satan. Indeed, the plot of Satan has ever been weak (Surat An-Nisa' 76).

So fight, [O Muhammad], in the cause of Allah; you are not held responsible except for yourself. And encourage the believers [to join you] that perhaps Allah will restrain the [military] might of those who disbelieve. And Allah is greater in might and stronger in [exemplary] punishment (Surat An-Nisa' 84).

They wish you would disbelieve as they disbelieved so you would be alike. So do not take from among them allies until they emigrate for the cause of Allah. But if they turn away, then seize them and kill them wherever you find them and take not from among them any ally or helper (Surat An-Nisa' 89).

A prophet teaches about repentance and purity, but Muhammad never taught or mentioned anything about sin. It was not even a matter to be considered. His life was sinful and focused on sexuality (including adultery), murder, and vindication. He depicted heaven as enticing and carnal with beautiful women and marriage. According to Surat Ad-Dukhan, 51 – 57:

Indeed, the righteous will be in a secure place; Within gardens and springs, Wearing [garments of] fine silk and brocade, facing each other. Thus. And we will marry them to fair women with large, [beautiful] eyes. They will call therein for every [kind of] fruit – safe and secure. They will not taste death therein except the first death, and He will have protected them from the punishment of Hellfire. As bounty from your Lord. That is what is the great attainment.

As for the end of the Prophet Muhammad, he was killed by a Jewish woman who put poison in some meat and offered it to him (Sahih Muslim, page 714).

After all that I read and studied, I recognized that the Prophet of Islam is not a prophet from God. According to the Holy Bible, a prophet must be sent by God to speak God's Word to people, not his own personal words:

> *For prophecy never had its origin in the human will, but prophets, though human, spoke from God as they were carried along by the Holy Spirit* (2 Peter 1:21).

6.   A prophet doesn't work for himself, but does God's work who is the initiator of the message:

> *As long as it is day, we must do the works of him who sent me* (John 9:4).

7. A prophet shouldn't set his own personal goals and agenda, but live in obedience to God's direction for his life:

> *"My food," said Jesus, "is to do the will of him who sent me and to finish his work"* (John 4:34).

8.   A prophet should live as a role model of holiness to the people he is ministering to, and not make them stumble:

> *We did this, not because we do not have the right to such help, but in order to offer ourselves as a model for you to imitate* (2 Thessalonians 3:9).

9.   The message of a prophet should be to help people to rise above their fleshly desires, and live by the Spirit:

> *So, I say, walk by the Spirit, and you will not gratify the desires of the flesh* (Galatians 5:16).

10. A prophet is a human being but he shouldn't indulge in immorality and other frivolous pursuits:

> *No, I strike a blow to my body and make it my slave so that after I have preached to others, I myself will not be disqualified for the prize* (1 Corinthians 9:27).

You can only imagine how devastated and upset and disappointed I was to read these facts about the Prophet Muhammad and Islam! My heart was breaking because I knew this was the beginning of much heartache for me. What about my dearest family who didn't know what I now knew? Should I *leave* them because of the truth I was finding out about our religion? Or should I continue to walk in the darkness even after what I learned? Should I only deny Islam in my heart but continue living and pretending to be a Muslim? How *can* I live as a Muslim after finding out the truth? How can I tell my family about this truth? What should I do now? I was too confused and hundreds of questions were filling my mind. There was a bitter war going on between my mind and my heart.

3

Following Jesus

Did Jesus say "I am God"?

Every devout Muslim is very committed to God (Allah in Arabic.) Muhammad may have been an ordinary person. The Quran may have been a human book. But the desire and longing of my heart and the heart of Muslims is to know God himself.

The Prophet Muhammad, who was the heart and soul of Islam, had been devalued in my eyes. Although I felt horrible, I wanted to know how to find a way to worship the one true God. I wanted to find out more of who Jesus was. Was he in fact the God who controlled my destiny?

One day as I continued to read the Bible, Jesus talked to me through Luke 8. As I was reading, the Lord touched my heart and quenched my thirst. The passage starts in verse 26:

110

They sailed to the region of the Gerasenes, which is across the lake from Galilee. When Jesus stepped ashore, he was met by a demon-possessed man from the town. For a long time this man had not worn clothes or lived in a house, but had lived in the tombs. When he saw Jesus, he cried out and fell at his feet, shouting at the top of his voice, "What do you want with me, Jesus, Son of the Most High God? I beg you, don't torture me!" For Jesus had commanded the impure spirit to come out of the man. Many times it had seized him, and though he was chained hand and foot and kept under guard, he had broken his chains and had been driven by the demon into solitary places.

Jesus asked him, "What is your name?"

"Legion," he replied, because many demons had gone into him. And they begged Jesus repeatedly not to order them to go into the Abyss.

A large herd of pigs was feeding there on the hillside. The demons begged Jesus to let them go into the pigs, and he gave them permission. When the demons came out of the man, they went into the pigs, and the herd rushed down the steep bank into the lake and was drowned.

When those tending the pigs saw what had happened, they ran off and reported this in the town and countryside, and the people went out to see what had happened. When they came to Jesus, they found the man from whom the demons had gone out, sitting at Jesus' feet, dressed and in his right mind, and they were afraid. Those who had seen it told the people how the demon-possessed man had been cured. Then all the people of the region of the Gerasenes asked Jesus to leave them, because they were overcome with fear. So he got into the boat and left.

The man from whom the demons had gone out begged to go with him, but Jesus sent him away, saying, "<u>Return home and tell how much God has done for you</u>." So the man went away and told all over town how much Jesus had done for him.

The words underlined above got my attention, and touched my heart. The Lord Jesus had exercised his full authority over Satan and cast him out of the man, but then he told him to go back home and tell how much *God* had done for him. Jesus didn't say to him, "how much *I* have done for you," but how much *God* has done for you." Jesus wanted the man to know that he was not an ordinary person, like other human beings. In his own words, Jesus was saying he was God, and he was proving it by his power over Satan.

This calmed me down a bit and helped me breathe deeply. It was an answer to the burning question in my mind, "Was Jesus God?" I think you could have seen the relief on my face, because, in this story, I could hear Jesus answering yes to my question.

Jesus also said, *"All authority in heaven and on earth has been given to me"* (Matthew 28:18). Who can be the one that has all the authority on earth and heaven but God and God alone?

The Conflict Escalates

One day a man visited the refugee camp, buying and selling gold at good prices. I wanted very much to have something with Jesus' picture on it, and I saw a religious medal he was selling of the Virgin Mary holding the baby Jesus. In the book of Luke in the Bible, I had read the following story about Mary:

> *In the sixth month of Elizabeth's pregnancy, God sent the angel Gabriel to Nazareth, a town in Galilee, to a virgin pledged to be married to a man named Joseph, a descendant of David. The virgin's name was Mary. The angel went to her and said, "Greetings, you who are highly favored! The Lord is with you."*
>
> *Mary was greatly troubled at his words and wondered what kind of greeting this might be. But the angel said to her, "Do not be afraid, Mary; you have found favor with God. You will conceive and give birth to a son, and you are to call him Jesus. He will be great and will be called the Son of the Most High. The Lord God will give him the throne of his father David, and he will reign over Jacob's descendants forever; his kingdom will never end."*
>
> *"How will this be," Mary asked the angel, "since I am a virgin?"*
>
> *The angel answered, "The Holy Spirit will come on you, and the power of the Most High will overshadow you. So the holy one to be born will be called the Son of God. Even Elizabeth your relative is going to have a child in her old age, and she who was said to be unable to*

conceive is in her sixth month. For no word from God will ever fail."

"I am the Lord's servant," Mary answered. "May your word to me be fulfilled." Then the angel left her.

At that time Mary got ready and hurried to a town in the hill country of Judea, where she entered Zechariah's home and greeted Elizabeth. When Elizabeth heard Mary's greeting, the baby leaped in her womb, and Elizabeth was filled with the Holy Spirit. In a loud voice she exclaimed: "Blessed are you among women, and blessed is the child you will bear! But why am I so favored, that the mother of my Lord should come to me? As soon as the sound of your greeting reached my ears, the baby in my womb leaped for joy. Blessed is she who has believed that the Lord would fulfill his promises to her!"

I had empathy for the Virgin Mary and her interesting story. When I read it, I became teary eyed because of the purity and kindness of this great woman who was willing, for God's sake, to accept the shame and rejection that would come from people who would severely judge a girl who got pregnant without being married. She knew this was a gift and a miracle from heaven, and obeyed God humbly and quietly.

I bought the religious medal for a good price and I put it on a golden chain around my neck. When my friend's mother saw it, she said, "My daughter, now that you have this medal, don't be ashamed of it. And don't just wear it in front of us Christians, and hide it when you visit your Muslim family. You must be proud of it everywhere. Don't deny Jesus Christ and God will protect you."

I took these words to heart. That weekend, when I went to visit my aunt, I had the medal around my neck, but I was scared. All the way, in the train, to my aunt's house, I prayed, "O Jesus, I am not denying you or your mother. I have you here around my neck, but I don't know what will happen when I get to my aunt's. I love you and your mother, and you will defend me. I want to start seriously with you but I don't know where that will take me."

In spite of my prayers, I was afraid of what would happen when my aunt saw the medal around my neck. After getting off the train, I started walking to her house and feeling more and more worried and nervous. When I got there, I could see that her welcome was very cold, and her usual love wasn't there. My aunt is the kind of person who loves those she approves of. She can't accept people who have opinions contrary to her opinion. When she saw me, she had her doubts about me but didn't know where to start with the questions that were filling her head. She was generous as usual in spite of the cold treatment she gave me. Deep down inside, she had a good heart, and we enjoyed a delicious meal she had fixed for the family.

After dinner, she asked me to go to the bedroom upstairs with her for the afternoon prayer. She wanted to see if I was still praying my Muslim prayers. With fear and respect, I agreed to pray with her. We went upstairs, put on the long prayer clothes, and I started to pray the Islamic prayers, while also talking to my Lord Jesus and asking him to forgive me. I said, "Lord, I'm lying in front of you, but I'm embarrassed and afraid, and don't want to make a problem now in my aunt's house."

I didn't read any Islamic verses during this prayer. After praying, we went down to the sitting room to talk. Suddenly, my aunt came towards me, seeing the medal of Mary and Jesus, she yanked it off my neck screaming, "What is this thing you are wearing? Are you mad? You have the audacity to wear these Christian things! Are you trying to challenge us? Did you become a Christian???" I said, "No."

She said, "You are wearing the Virgin Mary now, and soon you will wear the Cross." I reassured her that this would never happen. We had a long painful argument with lots of hurtful words, and I left her house and never entered it again.

But she did not drop the subject and she was not finished with me. She had her doubts and fears that I had left Islam and turned to Christianity. She called a friend of theirs who was a professor of Islamic Law (Sharia) in one of the universities, and that man invited me to a meeting and started to give me lessons in the Islamic Law (Sharia). After some time, my aunt called and invited me to lunch at her house, and told me that they wanted to talk to me.

However, I didn't want to go to that Islamic meeting, because I knew what they wanted. They wanted to bombard me with verses from the Quran and some of the Prophet's conversations which most Muslims don't read or know about. I knew that this professor was preparing a lecture to brainwash me. I knew they would say things against the Jesus that I loved but didn't know how to defend.

I refused to go and made excuses that I had too much to do at work and school, so my aunt got very angry and said, "You are not obeying my words." She angrily hung up, and I never called her again.

Jesus is God incarnate

In spite of all the faith I had in my heart in the Lord Jesus, I still had some doubts. I was confused about how God can be manifested in Jesus' body. I prayed for understanding but found that every positive step I took forward, I took two steps backwards.

But God didn't abandon me to my confusion. I woke up one morning to the sound of paper being shoved under my door. It was the mail and I was excited to receive a letter. But this time it was not a letter. It was a small booklet entitled "Jesus is God manifested in the flesh." I was amazed and said, "O Lord, how great you are! You answered my heart's request!"

I started to read immediately and when I finished reading, I was convinced that Jesus Christ was God. Here is the basic argument of what I read, which starts with the story of the birth of Jesus:

This is how the birth of Jesus the Messiah came about: His mother Mary was pledged to be married to Joseph, but before they came together, she was found to be pregnant through the Holy Spirit. Because Joseph her husband was faithful to the law, and yet did not want to expose her to public disgrace, he had in mind to divorce her quietly.

But after he had considered this, an angel of the Lord appeared to him in a dream and said, "Joseph son of David, do not be afraid to take Mary home as your wife, because what is conceived in her is from the Holy Spirit. She will give birth to a son, and you are to give

him the name Jesus, because he will save his people from their sins" (Matthew 1:18 – 21).

In the above verses, we have the fulfillment in the New Testament of God's promise made in Genesis 3:15: ***"And I will put enmity between you and the woman, and between your offspring and hers; he will crush your head, and you will strike his heel."*** Here in the beginning of the New Testament, we see this promise fulfilled in Jesus who is the woman's offspring. His coming into the world was not the result of a man's seed into a woman's womb, so he is not the offspring of a man, or another human. But He is the only person who was born through a woman alone, without the seed of another human being. So, the question becomes: "How did the blessed Virgin Mary get pregnant with baby Jesus?"

The answer is in the above verses*:* ***"She was found to be pregnant through the Holy Spirit,"*** and the result was the baby Jesus as a human being in her womb. This matter was above Mary's ability to understand. When the Angel Gabriel visited her to tell her was selected by God to carry the Divine Child in her womb, she asked*,* ***"How will this be, since I am a virgin?"***

The angel answered, "The Holy Spirit will come on you, and the power of the Most High will overshadow you. So the holy one to be born will be called the Son of God" (Luke 1: 34 – 35).

If we understand that it was the Holy Spirit of God that came upon Mary and made her pregnant, we can recognize the fact that the baby she carried in her womb had a divine nature. This was to fulfill another prophecy in Isaiah 9:6: ***"For to us a child is born, to us a son is given, and the government will be on his*** *shoulders. And he will be called Wonderful Counselor, Mighty God, Everlasting Father, Prince of Peace."*

In John's gospel we read more about the Christ:

> *In the beginning was the Word, and the Word was with God, <u>and the Word was God… And the Word became flesh and dwelt among us</u>, and we have seen his glory, glory as of the only Son from the Father, full of grace and truth* (John 1: 1 – 14).

These verses seem clear and simple: The Word is Jesus Christ, who became flesh—a human being living among human beings. The verse tells us that he is God: *"The Word was God."* The rest of the verses between verse 1 and 14 confirm this truth. The Apostle John, who wrote this book, was inspired by the Holy Spirit to write, *"<u>All things were made through him</u> and without him was not anything made that was made. <u>In him was life</u>, and the life was the light of men… He was in the world, and <u>the world was made through him</u>, yet the world did not know him"* (John !:3, 4 and 10).

Is it conceivable that a human creature can give life? No, only God in his glory can give life. So this fundamental truth proves the divine identity of Christ, and God is not trying to hide this from us, but he declares it in several ways, according to his superior divine wisdom. The Apostle Paul said:

> *Have this mind among yourselves, which is yours in Christ Jesus, <u>who, though he was in the form of God, did not count equality with God a thing to be grasped</u>, but emptied himself, by taking the form of a servant, being born in the likeness of men.*

And being found in human form, he humbled himself by becoming obedient to the point of death, even death on a cross (Philippians 2: 5 – 8).

We might ask, "Why didn't Jesus just come right out and clearly say he was God? Doesn't he know that there are people who want to know the truth?" The answer lies in the last verse quoted, which tells us that God, in his wisdom, emptied himself, by taking the form of a servant, and being born in the likeness of men.

In his divine wisdom, he knew that it was very unlikely for people to believe someone who claimed to be God. If a man says, "I am God," people will believe he is blaspheming. Soon that person would be outcast, despised and oppressed. Or people may think he's crazy or delusional. Jesus may not have clearly stated that He was God, but this doesn't mean that he didn't imply it in different ways with what he said and with the supernatural miracles he performed on his own authority. As God, he exercised authority over everything that existed on earth, including nature, people, demons, different diseases, and even death. In his teachings and conversations, Jesus showed this blessed truth over and over. For example, in John's gospel, we read about Jesus saying to the Jews, *"Truly, truly, I say to you, before Abraham was, I AM"* (John 8:58).

We know that the time difference between Abraham and Jesus was around two thousand years, so how can Jesus say, "I AM," meaning that he existed before Abraham? Jesus did in fact exist before Abraham considering he is the Holy God who made all things. Notice that Jesus said, "I AM," not "I was." He's indicating that he has existed from eternity past to eternity future. He is indicating that he is God. When God appeared to Moses in the burning bush, in Exodus 3: 13 – 15, Moses said to God:

> *If I come to the people of Israel and say to them, "The God of your fathers has sent me to you," and they ask me, 'What is his name?' what shall I say to them?"*

> *God said to Moses, " I Am Who I Am." And he said, "Say this to the people of Israel, 'I AM has sent me to you… This is my name forever, and thus I am to be remembered throughout all generations.'"*

So when Jesus said, *"Before Abraham was, I AM,"* he was saying that he was the same God who appeared to Moses. And now, this eternal God had come down to earth to save his people. Many prophecies were written hundreds of years before Jesus came to our world in human form, which were fulfilled at his coming. For example, Micah wrote 700 years before Jesus came:

> *But you, O Bethlehem Ephrathah, who are too little to be among the clans of Judah, from you shall come forth for me one who is to be ruler in Israel, whose coming forth is from of old, from ancient days* (Micah 5:2).

Paul, the Apostle wrote: *"Great is the mystery of godliness, God was manifest in the flesh"* (1Timothy 3:16).

Part III

Visions
and
Revelations

Divine Rescue

1

The Cross

This is the new understanding that I received through reading this booklet which God sent to me just at the right time. The God I was longing for was Jesus Christ.

Leaving Islam for good

From all that I was learning, I reached the conclusion that I must remove Islam from my life. Every time I searched and studied an issue, trying to find an excuse to defend Islam and prove that it was the true religion, I failed. I found instead that Muhammad was not a true prophet and Islam was an earthly religion. I found that the Lord Jesus was God, and in his hands were true strength and authority. My mind and logic dictated that I should follow the one who saved me and rescued me from hell, and my heart was getting more and more full of the one who was God in a body; Jesus, my beloved, who was so beautiful and humble, willing to heal all who come to him with one touch or one word. There was no doubt in my heart that Jesus was God, and that I completely believed in him now.

But I was still afraid of taking the final strong and bold step, because I still felt I didn't have the human strength to make this fateful decision and break with my family. It was a costly decision from all sides. My family, my relatives, my friends—all the people I loved and admired. They were all well-educated, but may God have mercy on the one who made a mistake in that family. I remembered that every time someone made a mistake or did a shameful thing, they would hang him on a high pole and insult him forever! They would keep talking about the story over and over, and slashing him with their knives in the family meetings, on the phone, everywhere. He would get exiled from the family and everybody would cut him off for good. Was I willing to lose the love of my family and endure slander, making my parents and sisters and brother the reproach of all the relatives?

Just the thought of this gave me bad headaches and nausea. I would tell myself, "Why do you want to create a revolution by following Jesus?" But the real sad question was this, "Why couldn't I choose Jesus as my Lord and my God without setting my life on fire?" I wished I could just do this thing silently and secretly, but the Lord Jesus responded with these words:

> *Truly, I say to you, there is no one who has left house or wife or brothers or parents or children, for the sake of the kingdom of God, who will not receive many times more in this time, and in the age to come eternal life* (Luke 18: 29 – 30).

I kept telling the Lord that this decision was too hard and I couldn't take the stress any more. I kept telling him, "I don't have the strength to leave everything and follow you!" But Jesus never left my side. These words were his answer from the Bible, *"What is impossible with man is possible with God"* (Luke 18:27). And, *"Whoever does not bear his own cross and come after me cannot be my disciple"* (Luke 14:27).

I cried to Jesus, "O Lord, does this mean that I can't be your disciple unless I carry my own cross?" I knew that carrying the cross meant pain and suffering!

A golden cross

That same night, I dreamt about an old woman selling gold crosses. She asked me to select one but I couldn't decide. All of them were so beautiful and sturdy. I finally selected a heavy golden one and hung it around my neck. Immediately I felt extremely happy. When I awoke, I ran to my neighbors eager to hear an interpretation of the dream. I saw an old woman we call Nana. She was a believer who truly loved God. I told her all about my dream and asked her what she thought it meant. She said, "Daughter, the cross means pain and suffering, because the cross is where Jesus tasted the worst pain. You have chosen to walk the path of pain."

I did not like her answer too much. I was hoping to hear something about joy and victory. Her words left me feeling scared and wondering what kind of pain I had chosen for my life. This did, in fact, turn out to be a prediction about my future path of pain.

Jesus visits me in the night

I forgot about the dream after a while, but I kept begging Jesus, in my prayers, to help me and give me the courage to get baptized by water. One night I prayed so desperately, crying to God, that I finally fell asleep soaking my pillow in tears. Suddenly, out of a deep sleep, I awoke and saw a light in the room. I raised my head and saw a brightly lit cross. It was wide but got narrow farther away. Jesus was standing on the intersection with his arms open wide to take me in. He said, "Come." But I hesitated and gave him one hand saying, "I want to come to you with my family." He said, "You'll come to me alone," and then he disappeared. I fell back to sleep and didn't know anything until the morning.

That morning I was so tense, and told myself, "No way, this can't be true! What I saw is only a dream and I need to forget it." A battle was raging inside me. I loved Jesus, but I was refusing to go to him and refusing to be baptized, and insisting that I didn't want to cut my roots from Islam. They were deep roots which defined who I was.

The next night, sometime after midnight, I felt a bright flash in front of my eyes. I awoke and again saw the light which was even stronger this time. Again, he extended a hand to me and called me to come. I started to cry and say that I wanted to take my family with me. "Indeed, you *alone* will come to me," he said. But I didn't go.

In the morning, I felt so bad and guilty for refusing to go to Jesus. I felt so much love for him because he had taken the time to come to me twice and open his arms to me, but I was plagued with a very strange, uncomfortable feeling. Here I was torn up with fear, anguish and heartbreak, trying to take such a foreign path in my life. I felt like everyone else lived their normal life, and I was the only one struggling with these strange things. Why did I have to be the one to face these difficult things?

That morning, I read, " My sheep hear my voice, and I know them, and they follow me" (John 10:27). I started to talk to my beloved Jesus, feeling a great deal of remorse for refusing his invitation. I began to weep uncontrollably and said, "O Lord, tonight when you come to visit me. I *will* give you both my hands and go with you."

I waited impatiently all day for night to come and Jesus to visit me. That night, I couldn't sleep, waiting for the light to come, but it didn't. And neither did Jesus! In the morning, I prayed sadly, "Why didn't you come, my beloved? Did you get upset with me?" I begged him to come the next night, but he didn't come again.

Deciding to be baptized

I kept praying and begging the Lord to come. "O Lord, I want to see you," I cried, but he didn't come. So I changed my prayer to, "O Lord, I want to follow you, and when you come to me, I will not disappoint you, but I will go with you. But please give me the heavenly strength I need to take the step of baptism."

Jesus didn't come, but I felt that he heard my prayers, because my resolve was getting stronger. I began to have a strong desire to leave Islam, and get baptized as a Christian. I woke up, one morning, full of the Holy Spirit and an overwhelming love for the Lord Jesus. I called Pastor Matthias and told him I had to talk to him about something important. He asked me what it was, but I said, "No, no, not over the phone! I want to see you face to face."

It was Tuesday night, the night we had a Bible study and prayer meeting, so he came and picked us up and I told him I wanted to be baptized.

Pastor Matthias joyfully screamed, "FINNNNNAAAALLLLY! The Lord has heard my prayers! Thank you, O Lord," and his eyes were filled with tears.

I started to prepare myself mentally for the ceremony—the burial ceremony! Yes, I was about to bury all my past life, die with Jesus, and start my new life:

> *I have been crucified with Christ. It is no longer I who live, but Christ who lives in me. And the life I now live in the flesh, I live by faith in the Son of God, who loved me and gave himself for me* (Galatians 2:20).

At that time, I was participating in a Spiritual Discipleship course with a group called "The Branches of the Vine," which started in 2003. Martin had arranged for us to be in this group which was led by a Sudanese pastor from a Muslim background. He was a godly anointed man named Pastor Wajde, and he was from Canada. I told him that I had decided to be baptized and he was very happy for me but said I had to wait for the baptismal ceremony which was to be held on August 31st, 2003. My heart was so full of joy that I painted a beautiful painting of colorful flowers. This was the first time in my life I had painted flowers. Usually I painted dark abstract things that stemmed out of my feelings of depression.

I attended my course of Spiritual Discipleship which was held near a city called Zaphola in the north of The Netherlands. The course lasted four days, then I returned home to prepare for the baptism. I bought new things, and ordered a bouquet of red roses from my

Christian Iraqi friend, Amera, who was working in a flower shop. She was so happy for me that she said it would be her gift to me and she would bring the flowers for the baptism on Sunday so they would be fresh. I spent the Saturday before the baptism in quiet prayer listening to hear the voice of the Lord Jesus. But my Jesus didn't talk to me. Instead he filled my heart with inexpressible peace and tranquility.

The blessed day came, and I woke up early to get ready. I put on a very beautiful white dress that my friend Karolina had lent me. I was going to my beloved without shame or fear. When I arrived at church, I found that all the arrangements had been made and many of my friends were there, even ones I hadn't invited. All of my friends from the Spiritual Discipleship course also came.

The service started with holy songs in various languages: English, Dutch, French and Arabic. All the Zending (Dutch Organization) sang a song to me and then I gave a short talk addressed to my father who was living in Iraq at that time. I wished him to know that the teachings he had taught me were not in vain, but had brought me to know the real God. After that, in my white clothes, I was baptized in water which indicates that I was buried with Jesus and raised up with him. I can't describe the joy I felt at that moment. All my friends joined in my joy, and came to congratulate me. I gave everyone a red rose and a card I had made for them to remember this blessed occasion.

The wilderness and a fierce war

I went home after the baptism carrying beautiful roses and several gifts. The news had spread in the camp that I was going to be baptized on that day and become a Christian officially. I saw a group of people most of whom were Muslims and the rest were Christians who were born into a Christian family but may not have had a personal relationship with Jesus Christ. They were looking at me contemptuously with frowning faces as if I had stolen something from them or harmed them in some way. I didn't know the reason for their scowls, but I greeted them with a smile and the usual "Peace to You". No one responded to my greetings. They gave me a look that said, "You are pitiful, foolish and horrible." The Muslims wanted to spit in my face, and strangely enough, the Christians were not happy with me either.

I had imagined that my conversion would at least please the Christians. I couldn't understand their sudden change towards me when they were just fine with me the day before. Only one old woman replied to my greeting of peace with a cold hello. I started to hear some very painful words spoken about me in the days to come. They said that they couldn't understand how a woman from a respectable family could take such a big step and change her religion. They said that anyone who so casually breaks with her family and relatives was not a safe person and shouldn't be trusted. Such a woman was a traitor.

The gossip hurt me deeply. I wanted to escape and fly away to a place where no one was, except Jesus, so I could worship him and talk to him only. He knew my heart and how much I loved him. The words of King David in Psalm 55:6 were a comfort to me: "Oh, that I had wings like a dove! I would fly away and be at rest."

More family attacks

I didn't tell my aunt that I was getting baptized, because I was afraid of her and the family. The distance between us had gotten bigger after I stopped going to her house on weekends. But my aunt didn't keep silent about her fear that I was plunging quickly into Christianity. She told my family in Iraq that I was not listening to her, that I had stopped seeing her, and that I was forming lots of relationships with Christians and going to church. She particularly told my uncle Issam because she knew how much I loved him.

I started receiving phone calls from everyone. My compassionate mother called me crying over the phone because she was afraid I was aligning myself to Christianity. She didn't know yet that I had already deepened my connection with Jesus, been baptized by water in public, and removed Islam from my life, but she still felt horrible at the possibility. Every phone call I received affected my internal peace because it was charged with pain, screaming, and crying.

One evening, my phone rang and it was my uncle Issam calling from Tunisia. I truly loved and respected that man, and of all my relatives, I considered him as a friend. It was Ramadan in October of 2003. Uncle Issam spoke to me calmly as usual, because he was a diplomatic person who worked in a high political position for many years, and was good at peacemaking. He was talking cautiously to me because he had heard my news from my aunt and had told her that he knew how to speak to me because she had a rough way about her.

He said this to me over the phone, and I agreed with him that my aunt had a tendency to be harsh. So he said, "I would like to wish you a blessed Holy Ramadan month, and hope you are fasting." I was afraid to confess that I became Christian, so I answered coldly that I was fasting. He asked me what was new and I knew he was trying to get me to talk without him having to ask questions. Soon he led me to talk about the Prophet Muhammad. I didn't dare to tell him that Muhammad meant nothing to me any longer, so out of respect to his feelings I told him that I had been having some objections to Muhammad.

Mockingly, he asked, "What is your objection to Muhammad, O professor?" I said how could Muhammad, when he was a 25 year old young man marry a respectable Christian woman, Khadijah, who was 15 years older than him? He submitted to the rules of a Christian marriage, but after her death he entertained himself with many other women. And especially when he was in his 50's, how could he crave Aisha, a child of 6 years old and wait for her to be 9 and then marry her. And how could he be caressing her in shameful ways according to what is written in Sahih Al-Bukhari, Sahih Muslim and Al-Seerah Al-Halabiya. She was just a child, playing with children, and the stories tell of him coming to her while she is playing with children her age. The children would be told to go out, and Muhammad would stay with her inside and play sexually with this little child, and then he would go out and let the children come back to play with her.

Was this the role model for all Muslims? I also asked how he could crave his adopted son's wife, and because he wanted to marry her, suddenly a verse would descend on him from heaven allowing him to marry her. The verse said, ***"So when Zayd had no longer any need for her, we married her to you"*** (Surat Al-'Ahzab 37).

I kept talking to my uncle who let me talk and talk. He listened until he couldn't take it anymore and he got angry with what I was saying. He finally scolded me, "Who are you to talk about the Prophet of Islam in such a way?" He started to insult me severely saying, "By what authority do you dare to talk this way about the

Islamic Prophet Muhammad? This is insolence, ignorance and falsehood. Your thoughts are all wrong, and you've been a stubborn girl since you were young. When you think you're right about something, you don't even listen to your elders."

He ranted for a while then hung up on me. I knew that he would be angry and cut off his relationship with me after this. So instead of talking to me tenderly as he told my aunt, and instead of correcting my thoughts, he hung up on my without even giving any convincing answers to my objections.

I knew that all of my family was like my uncle. I always had to listen to the elders without commenting even if they were wrong, for fear they would cut me off. They were ready to exclude even a son or daughter from their love and tenderness without sympathy and without even trying to help. Here was my uncle, who supposedly was the most reasonable one in the family. He talked to me one time over the phone and decided to disown me.

Even so, the conflict with my uncle Issam depressed me because I loved him so much. He was always the wise close friend I had in the family, and now the closest relationship with a family member ended from my life. I felt so much pain and sadness, and went to Jesus crying, "I'm in pain because of you, because I love you; you should have helped me. Why are you cutting me off from the people I love?"

Five Severe Blows

1. An Unfavorable Answer to Prayer

During this same period of time, I had met an old Dutch woman that I loved dearly. She was so tender towards me, prayed for me, and treated me like a daughter. When I experience real love from an honest person, I become extremely devoted to them.

It happened that she had a small accident at home that resulted in the possibility of having her right thumb and her right leg cut off. I prayed for her fervently and said, "Don't be afraid, Jesus will heal you." I had faith that Jesus was hearing my prayers. I visited her every day at the hospital in Zuid Plain, which was quite far from where I was living. I had to take a bus, then the Metro, then transfer to another Metro, and finally walk some distance.

One day I got there to find she had gotten worse. I saw the worried look on the nurse's face and became frightened, so I knelt on the hospital floor and started to beg Jesus with tears and shouts to spare her finger and leg and heal her. The nurse was taken aback when she saw me kneeling on my face and crying out. But the Lord had compassion on my friend and she felt better immediately. Her face looked like it was back to normal.

I had to stay away a few days, but on a cold and snowy Tuesday Jan. 27, 2004 at 7:00 pm, I went back to the hospital to visit her, expecting that she was much better. When I entered her room, I was shocked to find out that she had just come out of surgery. They had cut off her leg above the knee!! I cried and cried and cried. I cried to Jesus, "Why do you cause me so much pain? Why don't you hear me and answer my prayers?" Now I felt that Jesus, my beloved, was letting me down in a big way.

2. The Government Comes After Me

As soon as I returned home from the hospital, completely depressed, I found a letter under my door. I saw immediately that it was from the government. I was hoping for some good news from them, because at that time right after Saddam Hussein, the Dutch government was issuing a lot of immigration acceptances to refugees. I said in my heart, maybe the Lord wants to bless me after my great disappointment.

But here was another horrible disappointment! I quickly opened the letter only to find another great blow to my life: a rejection letter for my case from the immigration department!! Not only that, they gave me a warning to leave The Netherlands within less than a month, because the government hadn't accepted my refugee case and had closed the file.

I screamed a cry for help, and all the neighbors close by heard my scream, and came quickly. Seeing the official letter in my hand, I think they knew. I cried, "This can't be right! How can they accept all the other Iraqis but kick me out of The Netherlands? Why me specifically?"

At the camp, we were used to hearing every day about someone being accepted. I felt shame, humiliation and grief. Those neighbors who loved me were sad for me but most started to talk about me, "God knows what she did and he's judging her and kicking her out of the country."

My tears sent me to Jesus. I felt my life was destroyed and I screamed, "Be merciful to me, Lord, for I am in distress; my eyes grow weak with sorrow, my soul and body with grief." I became very weak and thin after this hard situation, full of despair and frustration. I couldn't think. I didn't know where I could go. I felt completely paralyzed. I didn't know then that it was a fierce war of Satan!

3. A Serious Threat

The next day, I received a phone call from my aunt threatening that if I didn't go back to my Muslim faith, she was going to come to the camp and humiliate me mercilessly in front of everybody. She threatened that she would bring other Muslim people to the camp with her. I was frightened as to what they would do to me. I thought I was in serious danger. I immediately called my friend Karolina. I was in such a state of total collapse that she told me to get off the phone and wait to hear from her. She would manage everything.

She called Van Herek, a good and kind old man from our church, who bought old apartments and houses, remodeled them and sold them. Van Herek knew me very well and agreed to let me live in one of his apartments temporarily so I can escape from the people trying to hurt me, until the church could arrange a more permanent place for me to go.

Karolina came the same night and took me to an old unfurnished apartment, because I was afraid my aunt was planning to come immediately to cause problems for me. I was expecting her to bring other Muslim people to force me to go back to Islam. I went to the apartment on a snowy night in January. I slept with my clothes on and tears on my cheeks, shaking from the cold, fear and stress of my impossible life.

4. *Painful News*

The next day, on January 29th, 2004, I received another crushing blow when my mobile phone rang at 8:00 in the morning. It was my uncle Issam from Tunisia saying, "Condolences to you. Your father is dead." I screamed loudly and painfully. I buried my head in the ground and kept crying for half an hour while my uncle was on the phone hearing me. My heart was burning. I hated my life. The whole world became black in my eyes. I didn't have anybody to cry with me in my grief. My father had died and I was living far away with no one to support me. It was the hardest situation I had ever experienced in my life. My beloved father had passed from this world, but he would never pass from my memory.

5. *Physical Pain*

It wasn't enough that I felt abandoned by Christ, that I was being deported out of the country, that I was huddled in an empty room fearing for my life, that I had lost my beloved father—I also had a large painful growth on the bottom of my foot. It made it very hard to walk. Even my body was fighting me! I cried constantly and nobody cared about me. I didn't know what to do. I was surrounded by problems.

Giving up the cross and contemplating suicide

After all of these impossible blows that nobody could handle and still continue living, I got totally broken—broken psychologically, physically, financially and socially. And I had lost my family in more ways than one. I felt like I was a pile of straw or an old piece of worn rag—a thing without value. All I could think to do was to end my life.

I looked up to heaven with a look full of despair and said:

> Why, O Jesus, do you humiliate me when I came to you with all sincerity? I came to you with so much joy expecting that you would raise me up, but you are destroying me. I am hated by the so-called Christians in the camp who can't believe that I came to you from my heart. And the Muslims want to kill me. And you are not responding to my prayers. You no longer love me. Even this country that is supposed to be protecting me has rejected me and they want to expel me. The father that I love is dead and I had no chance to say good bye. And I'm unable to stand because of my leg. Is there any more humiliation than this? Do you love me or hate me?
>
> What's happening to me cannot come from one who loves me.
>
> Or did I misunderstand, that I was your daughter? If I'm your real daughter, why don't you come from heaven and take me now? Why don't you save me from this life now? What's the point of living like this, totally broken and humiliated? I can only conclude that you don't love me, that you hate me! I should have never come to you. Why didn't you tell me that your way is so difficult? And walking this way is so full of fear? People who walk your way live a horrible life, full of humiliation and sadness. Walking your way, everybody hates me, humiliates me, turns against me. Are you putting me through a very hard test?

I kept talking to the Lord Jesus, admonishing him painfully, heartbroken and full of anguish. The following words of psalm 88 described my feelings:

> *O LORD, God of my salvation, I cry out to you by day. I come to you at night. Now hear my prayer; listen to my cry. For my life is full of troubles, and death draws near. I am as good as dead, like a strong man with no strength left. They have left me among the dead, and I lie like a corpse in a grave. I am forgotten, cut off from your care. You have thrown me into the lowest pit, into the darkest depths. Your anger weighs me down; with wave after wave you have engulfed me. You have driven my friends away by making me repulsive to them. I am in a trap with no way of escape. My eyes are blinded by my tears.*

In my pain I wrote the following poem

> *I scream to you with my soul O God,*
>
> *Why have you left me?*
>
> *You made them mock me.*
>
> *Why did you stand far away from me, and throw me into the fire?*
>
> *They are looking at me with doubts and wondering.*
>
> *You who are Holy have humiliated me.*
>
> *People are rushing to harm me.*
>
> *I wonder, why O Father have you forgotten me?*
>
> *Evil is eroding my flesh.*
>
> *O Lord God, please help me and listen to me.*
>
> *Lift these boasters off me.*

Catch my hand and protect me

From the lions' mouths who are waiting to devour me.

I was wearing a small golden cross on a chain. Hastily, I took it off and put it on the floor and cried:

> Forgive me Lord. I can't handle your cross. It's too heavy, and it's better for me to die and be buried, or go back to Islam where at least I'll have my family, and friends' respect and love. I can go back to my aunt's house and find help and tenderness. Now, I'm poor, outcast, scorned, and hated by everybody. No one has any pity on me.

Suddenly as I was praying like this, I had an overwhelming desire to kill myself. Thoughts like this were shouting in my head: "I'm on the third floor, and if I throw myself from the balcony, nobody will care or feel sorry for me. Everybody hates me except my poor mother and sisters, but they'll be sad for a while then will forget me." A deep sense of bitterness was overcoming me. I can't begin to describe it.

I started to drag my legs heavily to the balcony and I looked down. When I saw how high it was, I felt afraid and pulled back, but there was a loud voice in my ear urging me to die and be done with the humiliation, loneliness, poverty and that wretched pain that was drilling in my foot like a nail digging into my flesh.

I said, "It's impossible to continue with this hard path!" I saw below the balcony a hard rocky pavement, and thought that everything would be over in just one minute if I jumped. I was hearing a voice encouraging me, "Hey, do it quickly! Don't be afraid; jump! Be brave and end this misery you're in. You're in big trouble with no way out except to die."

When people draw themselves towards the true God, Satan will mount a vicious attack. That's what was happening to me with the devil speaking in my ear to end it all. Suddenly, my phone rang. It was Pastor Matthias who said he felt I was in misery and called to pray for me. I immediately joined him in prayer over the phone, crying and wailing! That godly man saved my life and immediately raised up the whole church to pray for me. The feelings in my heart started to calm down. I felt the comfort from the Lord come inside me like a wave. I felt like a very strong hand entered my soul and immediately all thoughts of suicide evaporated. I realized at once that all the thoughts that had been destroying me were from Satan who wanted to rob me of my peace.

I regretted that I had taken the cross off my neck, so I went back and put it on. Everything changed and I felt God's power again, except that the pain in my foot was so bad that I could barely stand up.

I went out quickly in my heavy coat into the very cold and stormy weather. The rain was coming down in sheets and the wind was severe. It was quite dark at that time and I was crying while hobbling down the street. No one could hear me because the storm muffled every sound and there was hardly a soul on the street. My umbrella was broken by the wind. Walking was getting harder and harder. It took me an hour to travel the 15 minute distance to the hospital.

When I arrived at the hospital, I was soaking wet, my leg swollen and in a miserable condition. When they saw me like this, they took me immediately to the examination room and gave me some medicines and creams to try to break up and drain the tumor. They said this was a temporary solution and that I needed surgery within two days because my situation was serious. I still had to get up and walk back home. It was the most uniquely horrible day of my life.

A visit from my aunt

My aunt had called me on that sad day when I heard the news about my father's death, and had requested to see me. This was even though she had previously threatened that she would come and create a great scandal for me. The situation was different now that my father had died. I still loved her from my heart, and especially at this time, was wanting to see her and console her, but I thought it was unwise to give her my new address. I was sure she wouldn't kill me because she had more compassion than that, but some of her fanatical Muslim friends may come and kill me because I had left Islam.

I agreed to go and meet her at my neighbor's apartment in the camp, hoping that when we saw each other and I hug and kiss her, she would accept my situation as it is. But my aunt was stubborn and completely unwilling to accept my leaving Islam. With a sore foot, I went and met her in the camp, and all she wanted to talk about was Islam and Muhammad. However, with the family sitting around with us, the situation was not suitable for the conversation.

I said good bye to my aunt, wishing in my heart that she could know Jesus or even ask me why I wanted to follow Jesus, what attracted me to him. I just wanted a chance to tell her why I gave my life to Jesus. I didn't want to talk about him without her asking, because she obviously had no desire to listen.

After this I continued living day by day with the Lord, expecting every day that the government would come after me and kick me out of the country. But I prayed about this daily and the Lord must have sent his angels around me because no one ever came to deport me.

Right then, my love for Jesus started growing and I couldn't stop it. In a moment, I had gone from the depth of despair to a strong faith and dependence on him. I was ready to be forsaken by the whole world and be with him, even in the desert, because I finally found my meaning in him and wanted to keep talking to him day and night and read his words without stopping. After the foot surgery, I went back home, and for about two weeks, it was even harder to walk or move, so I spent most of my time reading the Holy Bible.

When I went back to church on Sunday, everyone was consoling me for my father's death. There was still a great sadness in my life that my father had left this life forever without getting to know Jesus and without a chance for somebody to tell him about Jesus. When he died, I missed him because I hadn't seen him since I left Iraq in 1997, and was lamenting that I never got the chance to sit with him and tell him about the Lord. I knew he loved his God whom he didn't know. He was following Muhammad blindly away from the True God. I kept thinking of the letter that he sent me when he heard that I was in contact with Christians. He had said, "Don't neglect your religion. I'm sure that you are going to spread a big message to the world." When he said, "a big message to the world," he didn't know that my message would be about the real God, the Savior who had all authority in his hands, and without whom, no one could be saved.

145

2

Confusion, Doubt, and Indecision

Sondos and the fall

I wish I could say my life was perfect from that point on. In fact, I experienced another fall soon after. In order for you to understand what happened, you need to know about my best friend, Sondos. She is one of the dearest people in my life. We shared most of our life history together, from childhood until now. From the time we were six years old, our lives have been enmeshed together because her mother was a friend to my mother, and her father was a friend to my father. We went through elementary school, high school and university together. Our memories were one memory. Our thoughts were one thought. We shared all each other's secrets and talked about all of life's subjects.

Sondos' father was a non-practicing Muslim, the opposite of my father who was a devout religious extremist. Furthermore her father was a Shiite and my father was a Sunni. In fact my father hated the Shiites and considered them infidels, yet he did consider Sundos' father his friend. Not only was Sondos' father an infidel because he was a Shiite, he was also an infidel because he didn't pray the Muslim prayers. In fact, this made him a first class infidel. Although he had a place in my father's heart, my father was always inviting him to pray. Their friendship was based on love and the spirit of fun.

Sondos and I loved to read books, especially during our teenage high school years. We would read the famous foreign novels like Tolstoy, Charles Dickens as well as the stories of Ehsan Abd El-Kudous and Najeeb Mahfooz. Then we would sit down and discuss the books in details. Our families would get annoyed with us for spending all our time together. She was a real sister to me.

Sondos and I had a passion for learning. My father knew this and always encouraged me to teach her the Islamic issues that her father didn't even know to teach her. I would tell her a lot about the Prophet Muhammad's Hadith (The spoken words of Muhammad) that my father taught me. She loved to listen and learn. I would tell her the words she must repeat 10 times a day to increase her income, and other words to repeat three times after the Morning Prayer and three times after the sunset prayer to expel demons. I taught her words to protect the house from robbery that we repeat when we leave the house, and other words we say before entering the house, and others before entering the bathroom, etc...

I was encouraging her to do what I did, and not to follow her father who was away from Islam. She was a beautiful person who loved everything related to God. She was faithful and loved to live a moral life. When we were grown up we continued to meet about 3 times a week to discuss everything. We had a lot of disagreements in our opinions and many heated discussions, but there was always a deep love and devotion between us. I was very happy to see her growing in Islam. She started to keep the prayers, and read the verses and Hadith that she learned from me. In time, Sondos became very committed to prayer, more than anyone in her family.

After I left the country, however, our relationship became colder and more distant for a while, but our deep friendship never left my heart. I always asked my mother about her and in time found out that she had moved to London when I was in The Netherlands. I got her telephone number, and with deep longing, I impulsively called her. I was afraid of how she would feel if she knew that I became Christian. I tried to avoid talking about Jesus Christ, but she caught from my words that I was somehow different than before. She had doubts but she didn't dare to ask.

After she hung up the phone with me, she told her husband, trembling, that she suspected something and she was afraid that I had changed my religion. She started to cry. Her husband said, "Even if she did, why are you so sad? Leave her!" But she insisted on knowing and making sure for herself.

I didn't know what I had said, maybe a sentence or a word, that created such fears in her heart, but she called me the next day. Her voice was stern, and she asked me directly, "Hey tell me now, do you have any relationship with Christianity?" I was shocked and troubled. I kept silent for a moment and replied calmly, "Yes, I became a Christian, and I'm now following Jesus."

She screamed loudly, "You are officially crazy! You? The one that used to teach others to follow Islam? You, who taught me the Hadith and all the important prayers? I'm now the big tree that you planted years ago and I'm growing in my faith because of you. When I heard your voice, I was so excited to cheer your heart and tell you that I'm following the way of Islam, like you always wanted me to. I've memorized all that you taught me."

I told her, "No dearest, Islam is totally wrong, and doesn't offer salvation from hell. Every Muslim will taste the fire of hell. There is no escape from this and there is even a verse in the Quran that confirms this: *"And indeed each one of you will go down into it (Hell): that was, upon your Lord, a Decree which was unchangeable"* (Surat Maryam 71, Authentic Quran; Commentary Quran Literal Translation).

She became angry and said, "No, you're the wrong one and Islam is the truth!"

We kept arguing for several hours and the discussion grew into a severe dispute. She asked me to give her my address immediately, so I did. In a week's time, I received some books written by famous men like Ahmad Didat and others. I started to read things that shocked me about Christianity. For example that there is no unity among Christian churches on the issue of the praying times, and that they have different ways of worshipping. As a Muslim, we are used to having the prayers said at the same time everywhere. I considered this a basic requirement of religion because Islam is based on the form of worship without the essence of worship.

I also read a detailed intelligent argument against the resurrection of Christ on the third day. The Islamic roots were still deep in my heart even though I was growing in adoration for the Lord Jesus and I believed in him. I also had the serious issue of cutting off my Islamic roots and living the rest of my life without the treasured relationships with my family. How could I stand the memories? How could I manage the pain that I couldn't control, if I lost them forever? So I opened my heart to find a reason to return to Islam. These books were like a small door and a pale light that seemed to clear the way. I'm sad to say that I fell for it like a young senseless baby who finds a piece of chocolate or a small doll. I was deluding myself instead of holding on to the truth.

The fall from Christianity and return of the prodigal to Islam

I was reading for long hours, and liked the idea of going back to the past. I missed the Islam which was opening in my heart once again. Soon, I fell into the trap of the cunning devil who dropped me into a sea of illusions and doubts. I started to open the Quran again after I had closed it for a long time. I also returned to the ablutions, the Islamic prayers and fasting.

I fell deeply into the abyss. I told my friend Sondos and she was very happy because she had succeeded in returning me to Islam. Still, I didn't stop my love for my Jesus, not even for one second. I continued reading the Bible every morning. But my heart was troubled and my soul was not at ease.

An uncomfortable sadness and emptiness, and especially fear, began to overwhelm me. Fear of the future, and surprisingly, fear of people. I felt that I lost my circle of affiliations. I wasn't affiliated to a country, a religion or to God. I was just trying to convince myself that I was right in what I was doing. But I wasn't, and this affected my service at church. That's why I considered this as a big fall in my spiritual life, but Islam considered it like a lost son coming back to his father's house. I said to myself, "I worship the living God who doesn't die. I don't know the way to walk, but he can see my heart and mind."

It was time for the Arabic Summer Conference, which is held every year. The beloved brothers at the conference were so happy to see me, but they had no idea that I was living in trouble and instability. I would listen to the sermons and the hymns, but then go back to the room to pray the Islamic prayers. I wanted God to reveal himself to me in any way possible.

Of course I didn't want anybody to know that I had returned to praying the Islamic way. One of the conference women, whose name was Eveline, was sharing the room with me. She happened to see me praying the Islamic prayers and wondered what was going on, but she didn't say anything. I thought deep down in my heart that I was being loyal to God and relating to him in all possible ways.

After the conference, I didn't feel the same kind of joy that I had felt after my first conference. There was something wrong and I was longing for God to talk to me in a clear voice to lead me and guide me to his right way. I was begging him to visit me like a year ago. I was living in a daze like an unconscious person. I wanted a clear voice from God to tell me plainly the way that I must walk. My return to Islam was like a kind of anesthesia for my conscience. It gave me a sense of happiness and helped me feel more connected with family again. I missed the relationships I had and wanted to recover them.

The confrontation

Pastor Matthias felt that I was cold in the spiritual services. I was still responsible for the translation and preparing the Arabic hymns. We Arabs at the church were a small group so I was responsible for preparing some hymns from CD's. In the past, I used to come to church early and always prepared the hymns. Now, I was being careless and didn't care to prepare them. Sometimes I would give excuses for not coming. The pastor asked me about the reason for the change and the coldness. He knew it wasn't my normal way. We were living like one family, and were always talking about all the details of our lives without fear or hesitation. We were living like real loving brothers and sisters.

I don't know how, but Pastor Matthias found out that I had gone back to Islam and that my friend had sent me some Islamic books. He was shocked and was deeply affected. The next day, he came to take me to the governmental department for an immigration follow up (I was still trying to figure out my immigration problems.) He was responsible for me like a real father. On the way back, he started asking me a lot of questions. He stopped the car and started to talk to me sharply, "What do you think of a person who tastes Christ's love and knows the Lord Jesus, and after that he rejects his love? Listen to this verse:

> *It is impossible for those who have once been enlightened, who have tasted the heavenly gift, who have shared in the Holy Spirit, who have tasted the goodness of the word of God and the powers of the coming age and who have fallen away, to be brought back to repentance. To their loss they are crucifying the Son of God all over again and subjecting him to public disgrace* (Hebrews 6: 4 – 6).

152

And also there is another verse,

> **If they have escaped the corruption of the world by knowing our Lord and Savior Jesus Christ and are again entangled in it and are overcome, they are worse off at the end than they were at the beginning. It would have been better for them not to have known the way of righteousness, than to have known it and then to turn their backs on the sacred command that was passed on to them. Of them the proverbs are true: "A dog returns to its vomit," and, "A sow that is washed returns to her wallowing in the mud"** (2 Peter 2: 20 – 22).

I said, "Why are you talking to me in this way? Why are you giving me these verses and discussing apostasy? And why are you being rough with me today?" As I was asking, my heart was beating faster and faster like I had committed a crime. He said, "You are very smart, and you know what I mean". He didn't let me respond and continued, "I found out that you are reading Islamic books, and that you've returned to Islam and started to give up the Lord Jesus after you knew him, and tasted his sweetness."

I interrupted him immediately and said:

> I will never ever give up the Lord Jesus, because there is no person in the world I love like the Lord Jesus. I've loved him since I was Muslim before I decided to be baptized. The reason I got baptized is to be with him forever. Jesus is my great love, but my love for Jesus is one issue and searching for the truth is another issue. Please leave me alone. I need to figure out my priorities and discover the truth for myself. I need to be alone with God, to know about him personally. Please don't force anything on me.

Leave me for some time in my doubts. This is about eternal life and I must be accurate in my decisions.

So Matthias, this lovely man, didn't say anything but kept silent in pain and drove me back home. He thought that the seeds that he had planted had fallen on rocky soil, and I had changed my faith because of the horrible experiences I was going through.

Now, many Christian friends from other churches wanted to visit me for the purpose of helping me in understanding some issues, but I didn't allow any Christians to visit me, not the ones I didn't know well, and not even those that I loved and knew very well. I felt tired physically and psychologically in all respects. I was in urgent need to know the truth about God from God himself, not from any human being. I felt miserable and bitter and empty inside. I thought of how much my Muslim family would rejoice if I returned to Islam, especially my aunt. But the greatest longing in my heart was for the truth.

Divine revelations

I was like an infant who had finally learned how to walk and run, and then returned to crawling. I had gotten rid of Islam, and then allowed it to come back and interfere with my life like a dangerous disease.

Now, I wanted to get serious with the Lord. I began to wake up early, every day before sunrise, to the total Netherlands darkness. I would go into the sitting room and open the curtains to look at the sky. I felt more secure that way feeling that the Lord could see me from heaven and I could see him. I would light a small candle and kneel to pray. Then I would beg and cry and scream

154

for his clarity. I would put both the Quran and the Holy Bible on the ground in front of me and cry to the Lord loudly:

> Tell me now, which one is your book? Is it the Quran or the Holy Bible? Which is the one that you wrote with your own hands? Which one is the heavenly book that you sent to your people? In which book did you send your teaching to your creatures, Lord? Please let me understand and guide me Lord. Please! Don't leave me blind!

I would cry like this with pain and zeal, then I would pray to the Lord Jesus, and then I would pray the Islamic morning prayer. Then I would say:

> O Lord, have mercy on me. Is this the prayer that is acceptable to you or is it the Muslim prayer? Which prayer do you accept as a sacrifice? Which prayer pleases your heart? Will you torture me like this? Will your tender heart allow me to live this way?

Then I would end my worship time very tired, and go through it again the next day and the next.

First revelation: The church is God's house

I started to feel tormented because the days passed without any response to my prayers. God was not sending me a single word. I would cry loudly and insist:

> O Lord, respond to me clearly because I'm a naïve child and can't understand unless you make it clearly obvious to me. I want to know your heavenly book, and I want to know if my going to church is a work that you love or don't love. Is church your home and the place that you dwell? Please God, I know that you are near to those who come

155

to you in prayer. I know that you are eager to answer sincere prayer.

I realized that it would be very difficult to know when I got an answer to these vague questions. Finally, I decided to put God to the test. I cried to him, "If my going to church is wrong, please Lord, break my leg when I go. Then I can know clearly that going to church is wrong. I would rather live without a leg rather than displease you."

The day came and I went to church. I came home. My leg was fine. I took this as a clear answer from the Lord that church was his real home.

Second revelation: The Bible is God's real book

I felt that I found the way to get a clear answer from God. So I decided to ask the Lord another question. I prayed earnestly, "O Lord, I want you to deal clearly with me so I can have no doubt of your answer. Please, Lord, when I read the book that is not your book, let me feel like vomiting, like I want to get everything out of my stomach."

I was adamant in this request for help, crying and begging loudly. Soon, one morning, when I opened the Quran, I felt a strange feeling in my stomach and wanted to vomit everything out of my stomach. At that time, I had forgotten my request from God. But that night during my prayers, I remembered what I requested and said to him, "O Lord, I want to make sure of that feeling." So, for the second time, I opened the Quran again, and the same bad vomiting feelings came over me again. I was getting excited that God started to deal with me in a very clear way, and said to myself, "That means that the Quran is not God's divine book, but let me try one more time and make sure. Maybe these feelings are just an illusion."

Thanks be to God, he responded to me in a more clear way than the previous two times! When I opened the Quran for the third time, I wanted to vomit from the depths of me, and there was a clear voice from God in my heart. I was so joyful and grateful that the Lord had responded to me. Even though there was a sad nostalgia in my heart for Islam, everything was clear now. I knew the truth that the Quran was not the book of God, and that the Holy Bible was the real and true book that contained the true teachings of our Creator.

The final battle

O Lord, listen to my cries!

See my heart's pain and my eyes' tears.

Have mercy on me and hurry to answer me.

You are merciful to those who plead.

In front of you I pour my soul

And to you, I raise my prayers.

Like the smell of incense I give them to you to intercede.

O Jesus, I invited you into my heart

And there's no place for another there.

Help me please, as I need to be filled with you.

I will not allow anyone else to rule my heart,

For you are my soul.

Your voice let me hear, and other voices dim.

Fill me with you and contain me, and lift off all burdens from me.

Now I started to entreat the Lord Jesus, with tears and wailing, to confirm his words to me and give me something else clear and tangible. I was begging him to baptize me with the Holy Spirit and change my life from the roots.

One day in the early morning during my intense prayers and crying, suddenly there was an urgent knocking on the door. It was Janet, my neighbor who lived just below my apartment. She was still in her nightgown and looked frightened. When I opened the door, she barged in and asked, "Is there anybody trying to hurt you? Is anyone attacking you?" I said, "No. There's nobody here. I'm praying to Jesus. Why do you ask?" She said, "We heard you screaming and begging in a loud voice, and my husband woke up frightened and asked me to wake up quickly and go to our Arab neighbor upstairs. He thought somebody was attacking you and he wanted to call the police."

I apologized for the scare I gave them so early in the morning. She said, "Please take care and lower your voice the next time. Your voice was so loud that you woke up everybody in the building!" I didn't realize as I was screaming for God to hear me that my voice woke up the dawn.

A dialogue with Jesus

After Janet left, I said to Jesus my beloved:

Are you satisfied with that scandal? You are not hearing me, O Lord. Am I not valuable to you?" I knelt and buried

158

my face in the ground and cried, "My beloved, talk to me, let me hear you clearly. I have your love. I'm your little child. I want to know what is the Holy Spirit, and want to be filled and taste a measure of grace from you. What's missing in me, and what's wrong in my life that prevents you from responding to my request?

Immediately I heard my sweet Jesus talking to me, saying "Yes, there are things that don't please me." I asked him what those things were that didn't please him. He said, "You have a lot of music cassettes, dance music and worldly songs that do not glorify me." I was shocked to hear this requirement and quickly said, "OK, Lord, I will get rid of them immediately!"

I got up quickly and went to the cupboard where I had stashed all kinds of musical cassettes. I used to love the eastern dance music, and I had a big collection of the most famous singers and musicians. I even had a treasured complete album of Abd Al-Halim Hafiz (a famous Egyptian Singer during the 60's and 70's). Yet, without any hesitation or pain, I collected all the cassettes and CD's and threw them in the trash.

I returned to the corner where I had been kneeling before. I knew that he was waiting for me. I had found a superior love better than the love of my mother and father. I called out to him again, "Where are you my beloved? I've obeyed your command and thrown all that music away that displeased you. What else? Is there anything else preventing you from dealing with me directly and giving me your power?"

He said, "Yes, there's something in the house that prevents me from working in you." I asked him what it was. He said, "There is more than one Quran here in the house. The house must be cleared of these Qurans!" I stood up quickly once again and collected the three Qurans that I had. I wanted to throw them in the trash but I stopped, because the Muslim thinking was still part of me. The Quran was considered a heavenly book, and out of respect, I stuffed the books in a bag, quickly changed my clothes and went out. I didn't' know where to go or where to put these books. I just walked down the street without a plan.

Finally I thought the best thing to do was to take the bus. At the bus stop, I thought maybe I should just leave the books there, but then the bus arrived and I got on. My mind was totally confused on what to do. But before reaching Capilla A/D Ijssel station, which is the next stop from Krimpen where I lived, I got off the bus and left the bag in the bus.

I immediately took the next bus, rushing home to where my sweet Jesus was waiting for me. The minutes were passing so slowly that I wished a plane would swoop from the sky to carry me home so I could continue my discussion with my beloved. Of course the bus was delayed and I was getting disturbed, but finally I got home, and ran to throw myself on the ground in front of the big chair where I sensed him waiting for me.

You will receive power

I started again, "I came back to you my beloved Lord, and did what you ordered me to do. I got rid of all the Quran books from the house. Now, please talk to me, my beloved. Please tell me if there is still anything that displeases you in my life now? Please answer me."

160

I kept waiting, but I didn't hear his voice. Still, my heart was full of peace and comfort. I knew that my beloved had accepted what I gave up for him, accepted my obedience to him. I continued the next day entreating him, "Lord, I want to see you!"

I prayed and cried as I prayed, and suddenly I found myself being lifted up to heaven, full of a joy that can't be described in words. A light filled the room although it was dark outside. I began to dance as if I was a plane in the sky. My body felt so light and I felt an unusual power. I touched Jesus' love and tenderness.

I will never forget that day in my whole life. It was Wednesday Nov. 3RD, 2004. I knew that I had had a visit from the Lord Jesus. He lit the room and touched my heart, tongue, mind and soul. I felt that I was very strong and could answer any person who didn't know the Lord Jesus, and talk to them and tell them about Jesus.

> *But you will receive power when the Holy Spirit comes on you; and you will be my witnesses in Jerusalem, and in all Judea and Samaria, and to the ends of the earth* (Acts 1:8).

Yes indeed, I felt a complete change from the roots in my life and a great rebirth that day. On that same day, I had an appointment with the Pastor to take me to the police station to sign papers regarding my stay in the country. I had been doing this every week according to Dutch law for refugees. There had been a court decision for me to leave the country and my stay was not approved. It was very important for Matthias to come with me, to protect me and help me.

He was in the habit of praying with me before we started our conversations. He would then start talking about the news he had heard from the BBC broadcast. This morning, he asked, "Did you hear what happened in the United States today?" I said smiling, "No! I don't care what happens in the USA or anywhere in the world. I'm too happy today! I'm happy and I want to fill the whole world with happiness. I love everybody! I love all those people who spoke badly to me. I want to shout loudly that Jesus is Lord. He's the only God. Jesus is the King and you are the son of the King!"

Matthias rejoiced at my words and my unusual happiness and asked me what had happened. I told him about Jesus' visit to me, and how he dealt with me and filled me with power and joy, and how he spoke to me and proved to me that the Holy Bible was God's book. Pastor Matthias raised up his hands, praised and thanked the Lord Jesus, and with tears said:

> I thank you, O Lord, because you are good! I thank you and bless you Lord, for your wondrous dealings with your daughter. I thank you Lord, because you have treated her with tenderness and visited her and confirmed to her that she is going the right way, the way of truth and life. I thank you from the bottom of my heart because you responded to my prayers for her.

After that I wrote:

> *In a moment of indiscretion, Satan entered into my life.*
>
> *I believed him and walked with him and left you.*
>
> *He filled my head with illusions.*
>
> *When I listened to Satan and forgot you,*
>
> *How foolish I was, and I hurt and insulted you.*
>
> *But you hurried to me, my beloved!*

162

I came back repentant and gave you my heart.

Forgive me, My Jesus, for my confusion and ignorance.

I repent ... and in my heart, I proclaim you King.

I announce it publicly, and I place you above all the beloved people.

You're my King, God and joy.

Everything I have, I give to you.

You are the crown on my head,

And the eternal lover of my soul.

More confusion about the deity of Christ

Now, as I began to read and study the Holy Bible more deeply, new doubts entered my mind. I was reading verses that made me doubt the divinity of Christ. I found myself in confusion when I read this verse:

> **In his defense Jesus said to them, "My Father is always at his work to this very day, and I too am working"** (John 5:17).

What confused me was that this verse was showing two different people, Jesus the Son, and the God the Father. But before, I had been convinced that Jesus himself was God. Another verse added to my confusion:

> **As Jesus started on his way, a man ran up to him and fell on his knees before him. "Good teacher," he asked, "what must I do to inherit eternal life?"**

163

"Why do you call me good?" Jesus answered. "No one is good—except God alone" (Mark 10: 17 – 18).

Here Jesus himself was asking, "Why do you call me good?" I did not know how to interpret this verse. It seemed that Jesus was clearly saying that God is the only good person and nobody else. Therefore, this would imply that Jesus is not God. And these verses confused me:

I am one who testifies for myself; my other witness is the Father, who sent me (John 8:18).

Now this is eternal life: that they know you, the only true God, and Jesus Christ, whom you have sent (John 17:3).

Now, it seemed clear to me that the Bible was teaching that Jesus was not God. I was getting confused so I went to church and asked Matthias who tried for two hours to explain this to me, but I went home without understanding any of it.

There was a new church close to my apartment, which consisted mostly of people from Ghana. They were very faithful and wonderful people, and every time I had visited that church I had felt the heat of the Holy Spirit. They were always happy to have me join them. So, the next week I went there and asked them about these confusing verses. I had another verse that troubled me as well:

Men of Israel, hear these words: Jesus of Nazareth, a Man attested by God to you by miracles, wonders, and signs which God did through Him in your midst, as you yourselves also know (Acts 2:22).

These verses were making me return to my original belief that Jesus was a good Prophet and God was with him supporting him with miracles. I asked the pastor of the new church about these matters. He started to explain in detail and said, "Jesus has two natures, a human nature and a divine nature. He is the Son of God like it says in Mark 9:7: *"Then a cloud appeared and covered them, and a voice came from the cloud: 'This is my Son, whom I love. Listen to him!'"*

I was in a great need for a strong spiritual touch, and a clear answer to touch my heart. I started praying with tears and shouts, "O Lord, please talk to me. Teach me, let me understand, guide me Lord. Are you God, Lord Jesus? Who are you? Don't keep silent, O Lord, speak and answer me."

I felt weak and deeply troubled. I had hundreds of questions in front of me. I began again to doubt if I was following the right way, the right God. Was Jesus just a Prophet or was he the One True God? There was a strong attack from Satan troubling my mind. He was trying to enter me again and drop me into a well of doubts and torment. But my beloved Jesus did not grudge me his help. *"This poor man called, and the Lord heard him; he saved him out of all his troubles"* (Psalms 34:6). Yes, the Lord heard me.

The Lord Jesus spoke to me through John 1:1: "In the beginning was the Word, and the Word was with God, and the Word was God." Here the Word is so clear, because Jesus is the Word of God and a soul from him like I learned before from the Quran. And the Word of God is God himself. This verse calmed me down a bit and gave me some rest and affirmation. I read it many times that night and went to my bed at peace.

Believe Me

I woke up very early as usual to pray, and to ask the Lord to illuminate my mind. I was continuing in my reading of the gospel of John, and came to a passage which shocked me although I had read it many times before. This time, the words from Jesus were different to me:

> *Do not let your hearts be troubled. You believe in God; believe also in me. My Father's house has many rooms; if that were not so, would I have told you that I am going there to prepare a place for you? And if I go and prepare a place for you, I will come back and take you to be with me that you also may be where I am. You know the way to the place where I am going.*
>
> *Thomas said to him, "Lord, we don't know where you are going, so how can we know the way?"*
>
> *Jesus answered, "I am the way and the truth and the life. No one comes to the Father except through me. If you really know me, you will know my Father as well. From now on, you do know him and have seen him."*
>
> *Philip said, "Lord, show us the Father and that will be enough for us."*
>
> *Jesus answered: "Don't you know me, Philip, even after I have been among you such a long time? Anyone who has seen me has seen the Father. How can you say, 'Show us the Father'? Don't you believe that I am in the Father, and that the Father is in me? The words I say to you I do not speak on my own authority. Rather, it is the Father, living in me, who is doing his work. <u>Believe me when I say that I am in the Father and the Father is in me; or at</u>*

least believe on the evidence of the works themselves" (John 14: 1 – 11).

My eyes filled with tears when he said, "Believe me when I say that I am in the Father and the Father is in me." The Lord Jesus is always speaking the honest truth. When he said, "Believe me," he wasn't only asking Philip and the disciples to believe on the evidence of the works themselves, he was also saying these words to me, the wretched, miserable and arrogant child that was full of doubts in the King!

I imagined that I was talking to the Lord Jesus instead of Philip, and that he was telling me, *"Believe me. I'm in the Father and the Father is in me."*

I knelt and buried my face in the ground and cried, "Forgive me, O Jesus, Forgive me, O Jesus, Forgive me my beloved. I repeated these words many many times during the next hour. I felt heated and filled by the Holy Spirit, and I felt the divine assurance that Jesus was the One True God.

The Lord Jesus continued to affirm himself through his word— especially the following miracle in John 9: 1 – 41 which I want to share with you in full:

> *As he went along, he saw a man blind from birth. His disciples asked him, "Rabbi, who sinned, this man or his parents, that he was born blind?"*
>
> *"Neither this man nor his parents sinned," said Jesus, "but this happened so that the works of God might be displayed in him. As long as it is day, we must do the works of him who sent me. Night is coming, when no one can work. While I am in the world, I am the light of the world."*

167

After saying this, he spit on the ground, made some mud with the saliva, and put it on the man's eyes. "Go," he told him, "wash in the Pool of Siloam" (this word means "Sent"). So the man went and washed, and came home seeing.

His neighbors and those who had formerly seen him begging asked, "Isn't this the same man who used to sit and beg?" Some claimed that he was.

Others said, "No, he only looks like him."

But he himself insisted, "I am the man."

"How then were your eyes opened?" they asked.

He replied, "The man they call Jesus made some mud and put it on my eyes. He told me to go to Siloam and wash. So I went and washed, and then I could see."

"Where is this man?" they asked him.

"I don't know," he said.

They brought to the Pharisees the man who had been blind. Now the day on which Jesus had made the mud and opened the man's eyes was a Sabbath. Therefore the Pharisees also asked him how he had received his sight.

"He put mud on my eyes," the man replied, "and I washed, and now I see."

Some of the Pharisees said, "This man is not from God, for he does not keep the Sabbath."

But others asked, "How can a sinner perform such signs?" So they were divided.

Then they turned again to the blind man, "What have you to say about him? It was your eyes he opened."

The man replied, "He is a prophet."

They still did not believe that he had been blind and had received his sight until they sent for the man's parents. "Is this your son?" they asked. "Is this the one you say was born blind? How is it that now he can see?"

"We know he is our son," the parents answered, "and we know he was born blind. But how he can see now, or who opened his eyes, we don't know. Ask him. He is of age; he will speak for himself." His parents said this because they were afraid of the Jewish leaders, who already had decided that anyone who acknowledged that Jesus was the Messiah would be put out of the synagogue. That was why his parents said, "He is of age; ask him."

A second time they summoned the man who had been blind. "Give glory to God by telling the truth," they said. "We know this man is a sinner."

He replied, "Whether he is a sinner or not, I don't know. One thing I do know. I was blind but now I see!"

Then they asked him, "What did he do to you? How did he open your eyes?"

He answered, "I have told you already and you did not listen. Why do you want to hear it again? Do you want to become his disciples too?"

Then they hurled insults at him and said, "You are this fellow's disciple! We are disciples of Moses! We know that God spoke to Moses, but as for this fellow, we don't even know where he comes from."

The man answered, "Now that is remarkable! You don't know where he comes from, yet he opened my eyes. We know that God does not listen to sinners. He listens to the godly person who does his will. Nobody has ever heard of opening the eyes of a man born blind. If this man were not from God, he could do nothing."

To this they replied, "You were steeped in sin at birth; how dare you lecture us!" And they threw him out.

Jesus heard that they had thrown him out, and when he found him, he said, "Do you believe in the Son of Man?"

"Who is he, sir?" the man asked. "Tell me so that I may believe in him."

Jesus said, "You have now seen him; in fact, he is the one speaking with you."

Then the man said, "Lord, I believe," and he worshiped him.

Jesus said, "For judgment I have come into this world, so that the blind will see and those who see will become blind."

Some Pharisees who were with him heard him say this and asked, "What? Are we blind too?"

Jesus said, "If you were blind, you would not be guilty of sin; but now that you claim you can see, your guilt remains."

In the third verse Jesus said, *"Neither this man nor his parents sinned…but this happened so that the works of God might be displayed in him."* Jesus is the one who performed the miracle and returned vision to the man who was born blind. Jesus used sand to actually create eyes to confirm that he was the creator. When Jesus spit on the ground and made mud and put it on the man's eyes and told him to wash in the Pool of Siloam, this was a process of creating. You can look at Jesus' healing miracles as proof that he's the greatest human doctor, but opening eyes that were born blind is not healing, it is creating. So we are confronted with a great creator, not a great doctor.

After I read this great miracle I was assured that the Lord Jesus is God, and I had great faith and deep joy in my heart and soul. His word strengthened me and consoled me and affirmed that I did select the right way.

I thank God that he pulled me away from Satan's deceptions. He had compassion on me. I was raised in spirit after I read this story from John 9, and I kept reading this chapter for many days.

The revival

I am confident that all of the internal turmoil and struggles that I faced were the result of my love for this person called Jesus! My misery came from Satan's attacks. The misery of our world is all because of Satan who controls this present age.

I wrote the following poem to tell my experience:

> *The love of God is a struggle against the stream*
>
> *A stand in front of the fiery arrows,*
>
> *Sinking with him to the sea floor.*

Your name is put on the list of the shameful,

On a big panel over the house.

Your reputation is hanging by a nail

And everyone is tossing you into the dust.

You're deprived of your family

And are running like a fugitive criminal

Facing pain and evil.

You are treated contemptuously

Like a desolate owl without a beak

Or a destroyed house without a wall.

But the love of God is a stroll in the rain,

A tree bearing sweet fruits,

A garden full of flowers,

You need to make that your choice.

Real love comes only from the justified Jesus

Who hung on the cross , the cross of shame,

Dutiful unto death with honor.

Despite his aversive appearance.

Love like this creates a song in the heart

Because it gives you power and stability,

Refreshes your life with fruits.

It sooths your mind with peaceful thoughts.

His pain is always a beatification

I stayed in The Netherlands until 2006. My asylum case was still rejected, but somehow I was never kicked out.

Abiding in the vine

I attended The Vine Branches conferences which consisted of several groups of wonderful faithful believers, each in a different city. I was growing after every conference; we studied several subjects like discipleship, counseling, and leadership. We got deeper and deeper into the Word of God, and grew in our relationship with Christ.

We lived in our groups like a family, like the first churches in Bible times did. We were waking up early, praying and fellowshipping together, reading the Holy Bible, and gathering for meals. There was true love between the members of the groups. This is the true way religious people should live with one another in harmony and unity. We were also complying with the biblical model of going out two by two to tell people about the Lord Jesus. This was a beautiful period in my life.

My relationship with Jesus Christ was growing daily. I learned so many amazing things about the Lord Jesus and put my faith into every single word I was reading. The Word of God was growing like a tree planted in my heart. Those years were a time of great spiritual growth.

The basics of Christianity

Here are the major points of Christianity that have been like an anchor to my soul:

1. The Lord Jesus is God himself.

    This is the most important thing to understand about Christianity. He is God manifested in human flesh. He is not just a prophet.

    Because he is God, his words have full authority on earth. We see this in the following verses where he uses the words I AM to speak of his nature:

    > *"I am the Alpha and the Omega," says the Lord God, "who is, and who was, and who is to come, the Almighty"* (Revelation 1:8).

    > *Do not be afraid. I am the First and the Last. I am the Living One; I was dead, and now look, I am alive forever and ever! And I hold the keys of death and Hades* (Revelation 1:17 – 18).

    > *Look, I am coming soon! My reward is with me, and I will give to each person according to what they have done. I am the Alpha and the Omega, the First and the Last, the Beginning and the End* (Rev. 22:12 – 13).

    > *Philip said, "Lord, show us the Father and that will be enough for us."*

    > *Jesus answered: "Don't you know me Philip even after I have been among you such a long time? Anyone who has seen me has seen the Father. How can you*

say, 'Show us the Father'? Don't you believe that I am in the Father, and that the Father is in me? The words I say to you I do not speak on my own authority. Rather, it is the Father, living in me, who is doing his work. Believe me when I say that I am in the Father and the Father is in me; or at least believe on the evidence of the works themselves" (John 14: 8 – 11).

If you really know me, you will know my Father as well. From now on, you do know him and have seen him (John 14:7).

"I and the Father are one" (John 10:30).

Jesus is not only God, but he is life and the giver of life.

For just as the Father raises the dead and gives them life, even so the Son gives life to whom he is pleased to give it (John 5:21).

In him was life, and that life was the light of all mankind (John 4:1).

Jesus answered, "I am the way and the truth and the life. No one comes to the Father except through me" (John 14:6).

Jesus said to her, "I am the resurrection and the life. The one who believes in me will live, even though they die" (John 11:25).

For the bread of God is the bread that comes down from heaven and gives life to the world (John 6:33).

2. Without the Lord Jesus there is no life.

    > *Whoever has the Son has life; whoever does not have the Son of God does not have life* (1 John 5:12).

    > *This is how God showed his love among us: He sent his one and only Son into the world that we might live through him* (1 John 4:9).

3. Eternal life is found through faith in the Lord Jesus.

    > *Whoever believes in the Son has eternal life, but whoever rejects the Son will not see life, for God's wrath remains on them* (John 3:36).

    > *My sheep listen to my voice; I know them, and they follow me. I give them eternal life, and they shall never perish; no one will snatch them out of my hand* (John 10:27 – 28).

4. The Lord Jesus gives life to those he chooses.

    > *For just as the Father raises the dead and gives them life, even so the Son gives life to whom he is pleased to give it* (John 5:21).

    > *Whoever eats my flesh and drinks my blood has eternal life, and I will raise them up at the last day* (John 6:54).

We read Jesus saying that he gives life and will raise the dead, but it's not just words. He confirmed these words by actually raising three people from the dead when he was on earth.

And anyone who can raise the dead is indeed the final authority over all things and the judge of all.

I will share two stories in which Jesus raised the dead. The first passage describes Jesus raising a little girl from the dead:

> *As Jesus was saying this, the leader of a synagogue came and knelt before him. "My daughter has just died," he said, "but you can bring her back to life again if you just come and lay your hand on her."* So Jesus and his disciples got up and went with him.
>
> *When Jesus arrived at the official's home, he saw the noisy crowd and heard the funeral music. "Get out!" he told them. "The girl isn't dead; she's only asleep." But the crowd laughed at him. After the crowd was put outside, however, Jesus went in and took the girl by the hand, and she stood up! The report of this miracle swept through the entire countryside* (Matt 9: 18 – 26).

The second passage describes the most incredible miracle Jesus ever performed when he raised a man called Lazarus who had been dead for four days and stinking in the grave.

> *Now a man named Lazarus was sick. He was from Bethany, the village of Mary and her sister Martha. So the sisters sent word to Jesus, "Lord, the one you love is sick."*
>
> *When he heard this, Jesus said, "This sickness will not end in death. No, it is for God's glory so that God's Son may be glorified through it." Now Jesus loved Martha and her sister and Lazarus. So when he heard that Lazarus was sick, he stayed where he was two*

more days, and then he said to his disciples, "Let us go back to Judea."

"But Rabbi," they said, "a short while ago the Jews there tried to stone you, and yet you are going back?"

Jesus answered, "Are there not twelve hours of daylight? Anyone who walks in the daytime will not stumble, for they see by this world's light. It is when a person walks at night that they stumble, for they have no light."

After he had said this, he went on to tell them, "Our friend Lazarus has fallen asleep; but I am going there to wake him up."

His disciples replied, "Lord, if he sleeps, he will get better." Jesus had been speaking of his death, but his disciples thought he meant natural sleep.

So then he told them plainly, "Lazarus is dead, and for your sake I am glad I was not there, so that you may believe. But let us go to him."

Then Thomas (also known as Didymus) said to the rest of the disciples, "Let us also go, that we may die with him."

On his arrival, Jesus found that Lazarus had already been in the tomb for four days. Now Bethany was less than two miles from Jerusalem, and many Jews had come to Martha and Mary to comfort them in the loss of their brother. When Martha heard that Jesus was coming, she went out to meet him, but Mary stayed at home. "Lord," Martha said to Jesus, "if you had been here, my brother would not have died. But I *know that even now God will give you whatever you ask."*

Jesus said to her, "Your brother will rise again."

Martha answered, "I know he will rise again in the resurrection at the last day."

Jesus said to her, "I am the resurrection and the life. The one who believes in me will live, even though they die; and whoever lives by believing in me will never die. Do you believe this?"

"Yes, Lord," she replied, "I believe that you are the Messiah, the Son of God, who is to come into the world."

After she had said this, she went back and called her sister Mary aside. "The Teacher is here," she said, "and is asking for you." When Mary heard this, she got up quickly and went to him. Now Jesus had not yet entered the village, but was still at the place where Martha had met him. When the Jews who had been with Mary in the house, comforting her, noticed how quickly she got up and went out, they followed her, supposing she was going to the tomb to mourn there.

When Mary reached the place where Jesus was and saw him, she fell at his feet and said, "Lord, if you had been here, my brother would not have died."

When Jesus saw her weeping, and the Jews who had come along with her also weeping, he was deeply moved in spirit and troubled. "Where have you laid him?" he asked.

179

"Come and see, Lord," they replied. Jesus wept. Then the Jews said, "See how he loved him!"

But some of them said, "Could not he who opened the eyes of the blind man have kept this man from dying?"

Jesus, once more deeply moved, came to the tomb. It was a cave with a stone laid across the entrance. "Take away the stone," he said.

"But, Lord," said Martha, the sister of the dead man, "by this time there is a bad odor, for he has been there four days."

Then Jesus said, "Did I not tell you that if you believe, you will see the glory of God?" So they took away the stone. Then Jesus looked up and said, "Father, I thank you that you have heard me. I knew that you always hear me, but I said this for the benefit of the people standing here, that they may believe that you sent me." When he had said this, Jesus called in a loud voice, "Lazarus, come out!" The dead man came out, his hands and feet wrapped with strips of linen, and a cloth around his face. Jesus said to them, "Take off the grave clothes and let him go." Therefore many of the Jews who had come to visit Mary, and had seen what Jesus did, believed in him (John 11: 1 – 45).

Notice that Jesus said about himself that he is the resurrection and the life. Faith in him is the only way to life because he is the life giver who gives life to anybody who comes to him by faith. And what he gives, no one can take away from his hands. By these miracles he confirms that he is the true God who came to earth in human flesh to give life from physical and spiritual death.

5. Jesus gives comfort and rest to people and carries their pain.

> *Come to me, all you who are weary and burdened, and I will give you rest* (Matthew 11:28).

6. Jesus answers prayers that are offered in his name.

> *And I will do whatever you ask in my name, so that the Father may be glorified in the Son* (John 14:13).

Prayer in Jesus' name and according to his purposes will give strength in the believer's life to do great works, to bring healing, strength and power over demons.

7. Life with the Lord Jesus requires leaving everything else.

> *Anyone who loves their father or mother more than me is not worthy of me; anyone who loves their son or daughter more than me is not worthy of me. Whoever does not take up their cross and follow me is not worthy of me. Whoever finds their life will lose it, and whoever loses their life for my sake will find it* (Matthew 10: 37 – 39).

This passage was very important to me because it taught me that the Lord Jesus wants me to love him more than anything in the world, more than my family *and* even more than myself. In return, I have the joy of drinking in his great love which gives me true life and meaning day after day.

8. The Holy Spirit that gives power is the Spirit of God.

As a Muslim, I had never heard of the Holy Spirit. I learned that God is three persons, the Father, Son, and Holy Spirit. God said in the Holy Bible:

> *I am the Lord your God and there is none else. And my people shall never again be put to shame. And it shall come to pass afterward, that I will pour out my Spirit on all flesh* (Joel 2: 27 – 28).

> *When you send forth your Spirit, they are created, and you renew the face of the ground* (Psalm 104:30).

> *And the Spirit of God was hovering over the face of the waters* (Genesis 1:2).

Besides all that, I found that the Lord Jesus confirms that he will send God's Spirit:

> *But when the Helper comes, whom I will send to you from the Father, the Spirit of truth, who proceeds from the Father, he will bear witness about me* (John 15:26).

> *But in fact, it is best for you that I go away, because if I don't, the Advocate won't come. If I do go away, then I will send him to you* (John 16:7).

The question is: How can the Holy Spirit control God's Spirit if he is not God? The Spirit of God is the Spirit of the Son of God. This is what the Bible affirms when it says,

> *You, however, are not in the flesh but in the Spirit, if in fact the Spirit of God dwells in you. Anyone who*

182

does not have the Spirit of Christ does not belong to him (Romans 8:9).

Here he uses the Spirit of God and the Spirit of Christ interchangeably. If this is not clear, consider this verse which tells us who has guided the real prophets of God throughout human history:

> *For no prophecy was ever produced by the will of man, but men spoke from God as they were carried along by the Holy Spirit* (2 Peter 1:21).

The interesting thing that I learned is that the Holy Scripture confirms that he is the Spirit of the Son of God as well:

> *...obtaining the outcome of your faith, the salvation of your souls. Concerning this salvation, the prophets who prophesied about the grace that was to be yours searched and inquired carefully, inquiring what person or time the Spirit of Christ in them was indicating when he predicted the sufferings of Christ and the subsequent glories* (1 Peter 1: 9 – 11).

And because the Holy Spirit is the same Spirit of Christ, he therefore breathes the Spirit on the disciples:

> *And when he had said this, he breathed on them and said to them, "Receive the Holy Spirit"* (John 20:22).

So, who can give God's Spirit but God himself? Jesus says clearly, *"You are in me, Father, and I am in you"* (John 17:21). The work of the Holy Spirit is described here: *"He will glorify me, for he will take what is mine and declare it to you"* (John 16:14). The Spirit of God takes from Jesus and declares it

183

to us, so it is God's Holy Spirit who spoke to the prophets. He guided them in everything and gave them their unique message.

3

Why I Had to Leave Islam

There is a big difference between the teachings of the Holy Bible and the Quran—a difference as big as the difference between heaven and earth. There's also a big difference between the character and the life of Jesus and that of Muhammad. Everyone who cares about serving God needs to consider these facts.

1. Jesus taught forgiveness and not retaliation. He said,

> *You have heard that it was said, 'An eye for an eye and a tooth for a tooth.' But I say to you, do not resist the one who is evil. But if anyone slaps you on the right cheek, turn to him the other also* (Matthew 5: 38 – 39).

But the Prophet of Islam taught revenge.

*[Fighting in] the sacred month is for [aggression committed in] the sacred month, and for [all] violations is legal retribution. So whoever has assaulted you, then assault him in the same way that he has assaulted you. And fear Allah and know that Allah is with those who fear Him (*Surat Al-Baqarah 194).

2. Jesus was without sin.

He committed no sin, neither was deceit found in his mouth (1 Peter 2:22).

Which one of you convicts me of sin? (John 8:46).

Even the Quran says that Jesus did not sin.

But the Prophet Muhammad was touched by the Devil.

...because every baby must be touched by the Devil... except Issa the son of Mariam and his mother.

This is a Hadith by Muhammad quoted by senior Muslim scholars like Al-Bukhari (Sahih Al-Bukhari page/number 3286).

3. The words of Jesus Christ never change.

Heaven and earth will pass away, but my words will not pass away (Matthew 24:35).

But the words of the Prophet and the Quran fluctuate:

And when We substitute a verse in place of a verse - and Allah is most knowing of what He sends down - they say, "You, [O Muhammad], are but an inventor [of lies]." But most of them do not know (Surat An-Nahl 101).

4. Jesus Christ drove the devil away.

Again, the devil took him to a very high mountain and showed him all the kingdoms of the world and their splendor. "All this I will give you," he said, "if you will bow down and worship me."

Jesus said to him, "Away from me, Satan! For it is written: 'Worship the Lord your God, and serve him only.' "

Then the devil left him, and angels came and attended him (Matthew 4: 8 – 11).

Here is a story that shows the Lord Jesus casting out demons:

Just then a man in their synagogue who was possessed by an impure spirit cried out, "What do you want with us, Jesus of Nazareth? Have you come to destroy us? I know who you are—the Holy One of God!"

"Be quiet!" said Jesus sternly. "Come out of him!" The impure spirit shook the man violently and came out of him with a shriek.

The people were all so amazed that they asked each other, "What is this? A new teaching, and with authority! He even gives orders to impure spirits and they obey him" (Mark 1: 23 – 27).

Here is another story showing the authority of the Lord Jesus over impure spirits:

> *When he arrived at the other side in the region of the Gadarenes, two demon-possessed men coming from the tombs met him. They were so violent that no one could pass that way. "What do you want with us, Son of God?" they shouted. "Have you come here to torture us before the appointed time?"*
>
> *Some distance from them a large herd of pigs was feeding. The demons begged Jesus, "If you drive us out, send us into the herd of pigs."*
>
> *He said to them, "Go!" So they came out and went into the pigs, and the whole herd rushed down the steep bank into the lake and died in the water* (Matthew 8: 28 – 32).

Also, the Devil has no authority over Jesus

> *I will not say much more to you, for the prince of this world is coming. He has no hold over me* (John 14:30).

But the Prophet of Islam communed with spirits:

> *And behold we dispatched to you a group from the Jinns (demons), listening to the Quran: so when they attended to it, they said, "Listen quietly," so when it (the reciting) was over, they turned back to their people, to warn* (Surat Al-'Ahqaf 29).

5. Jesus healed the eyes of the blind man.

> *As Jesus approached Jericho, a blind man was sitting by the roadside begging. When he heard the crowd*

going by, he asked what was happening. They told him, "Jesus of Nazareth is passing by."

He called out, "Jesus, Son of David, have mercy on me!" Those who led the way rebuked him and told him to be quiet, but he shouted all the more, "Son of David, have mercy on me!"

Jesus stopped and ordered the man to be brought to him. When he came near, Jesus asked him, "What do you want me to do for you?"

"Lord, I want to see," he replied.

Jesus said to him, "Receive your sight; your faith has healed you." Immediately he received his sight and followed Jesus, praising God. When all the people saw it, they also praised God (Luke 18: 35 – 43).

But the Prophet of Islam turned his face away from the blind man:

The Prophet frowned and turned away. Because there came to him the blind man, [interrupting]. But what would make you perceive, [O Muhammad], that perhaps he might be purified. Or be reminded and the remembrance would benefit him? As for he who thinks himself without need, To him you give attention. And not upon you [is any blame] if he will not be purified. But as for he who came to you striving [for knowledge] While he fears [Allah], From him you are distracted. From him you are distracted (Surat 'Abasa 1 – 10).

189

6. The Lord Jesus sanctified marriage and called for monogamy.

> *Some Pharisees came and tested him by asking, "Is it lawful for a man to divorce his wife?"*
>
> *"What did Moses command you?" he replied.*
>
> *They said, "Moses permitted a man to write a certificate of divorce and send her away."*
>
> *"It was because your hearts were hard that Moses wrote you this law," Jesus replied. "But at the beginning of creation God made them male and female. For this reason a man will leave his father and mother and be united to his wife, and the two will become one flesh. So they are no longer two, but one flesh. Therefore what God has joined together, let no one separate"* (Mark 10: 1 – 9).

But Muhammad called for polygamy:

> *And if you fear that you will not deal justly with the orphan girls, then marry those that please you of [other] women, two or three or four. But if you fear that you will not be just, then [marry only] one or those your right hand possesses. That is more suitable that you may not incline [to injustice]* (Surat An-Nisa' 3).

7. Jesus came to save people.

> *Because the Son of Man did not come to destroy men's lives, but to save* (Luke 9:56).

But Muhammad called for killing people:

So fight, [O Muhammad], in the cause of Allah ; you are not held responsible except for yourself. And encourage the believers [to join you] that perhaps Allah will restrain the [military] might of those who disbelieve. And Allah is greater in might and stronger in [exemplary] punishment (Surat An-Nisa' 84).

Fighting has been enjoined upon you while it is hateful to you. But perhaps you hate a thing and it is good for you; and perhaps you love a thing and it is bad for you. And Allah Knows, while you know not (Surat Al-Baqarah 216).

8. Jesus is the Son of God. He is God appearing in the flesh.

And without controversy great is the mystery of godliness: God was manifest in the flesh (1 Timothy 3:16).

Why do you call it blasphemy when I say, 'I am the Son of God'? After all, the Father set me apart and sent me into the world (John 10:36).

The angel replied, "The Holy Spirit will come upon you, and the power of the Most High will overshadow you. So the baby to be born will be holy, and he will be called the Son of God" (Luke 1:35).

But Muhammad was a human being, a son of a man and a woman.

Say, "I am only a man like you..." (Surat Al-Kahf 110).

9. Jesus knew and foretold the future.

> *After they gathered again in Galilee, Jesus told them, "The Son of Man is going to be betrayed into the hands of his enemies. He will be killed, but on the third day he will be raised from the dead." And the disciples were filled with grief* (Matthew 17: 22 – 23).

This verse was fulfilled exactly as Jesus predicted. They caught Jesus and released him into the hands of the people, as we read in Matthew 27:26. Then after his death, he rose from the grave on the third day (as we read in Matthew chapter 28.) Jesus also told the people what would happen in their lives:

> *The time is coming when all these things will be completely demolished. Not one stone will be left on top of another!* (Luke 21:6).

This verse was fulfilled just over thirty years later, when Titus the Roman attacked the Jews and destroyed the temple and the walls of Jerusalem.

But Muhammad was unable to know the future or what was in people's hearts:

> *And I do not tell you that I have the depositories [containing the provision] of Allah or that I know the unseen nor do I tell you that I am an angel* (Surat Hud 31).

10. Jesus gave people the freedom to accept his message or reject it.

> *But if a town refuses to welcome you, go out into its streets and say, 'We wipe even the dust of your town from our feet to show that we have abandoned you to your fate. And know this—the Kingdom of God is near!'* (Luke 10: 10 – 11).

But Muhammad forced people to accept his message:

> *Fight those who do not believe in Allah or in the Last Day and who do not consider unlawful what Allah and His Messenger have made unlawful and who do not adopt the religion of truth from those who were given the Scripture - [fight] until they give the jizyah (tax) willingly while they are humbled* (Surat At-Tawbah 29).

11. Jesus taught his followers to give.

> *Give, and you will receive. Your gift will return to you in full—pressed down, shaken together to make room for more, running over, and poured into your lap. The amount you give will determine the amount you get back* (Luke 6:38).

But Muhammad taught his followers to take:

> *Take, [O, Muhammad], from their wealth a charity by which you purify them and cause them increase* (Surat At-Tawbah 103).

Additional information about Islam:

The requirements of Islam are that a Muslim must pray, fast, read the Quran (even if he doesn't understand the meaning of what he's reading), pay the Zakah (part of the income), and go at least one time to Al-Hajj (pilgrimage). If he can go to Al-Omrah, that would be best.

Islam is a masculine religion and supports men and gives them more authority by definition. The Muslim man has much more freedom than the Muslim woman, as the Islamic law allows men to do whatever they want in terms of relationships with women. For Shiites, there is a special kind of marriage called "Temporary Marriage for Entertainment," which is an Islamic Law that allows adultery for the sake of men being able to entertain themselves with any woman they want. It is done by saying a sentence, agreeing on a small dowry, and agreeing on the marriage period, even if it is a few hours. This is considered marriage. I think anyone can see what a hypocritical teaching this is; how adultery and marriage are contradictory.

A woman must wear the Hijab (head covering) to be considered a respectable and good woman in the eyes of society. It doesn't really matter what she does in private. Even if she doesn't pray or even if she is a nosy gossip, she is respectable as long she covers her hair. Now, if she is sinning and her bad character becomes known, she will be humiliated by society, but she can be forgiven if she repents. If she doesn't repent, she will have much trouble. Yet, even this sinful woman is considered better than another woman who is holy and pure but has left Islam to become a Christian. The first woman has bad morals, but at least she's a

Muslim woman. The second one is considered an infidel. This is how they consider me. I was now an infidel in the eyes of my family and friends, but should a person seek the approval of family over the approval of God? I could never do that.

Part IV

Divine
Rescue

1

Leveling the Mountains

Message from Heaven

The Lord Jesus is tender and merciful. Although he may allow some tests for his sons and daughters in order to purify and discipline them, he always comes through when a person is hopelessly at the end of his rope. I was at this time coming to the end of my rope with regards to staying in The Netherlands.

It was the year 2006, and the situation with my immigration was at the end stages—my file had been denied, and I had to leave the country. But my soul was at rest and I had the faith that the Lord Jesus would not leave me nor forsake me.

I concentrated my efforts on learning about the Lord. I read the story of the Apostle Paul when the Lord Jesus appeared to him and turned his life around and transformed his heart from a hard to a soft one. Immediately he started to preach Christ: *"At once he began to preach in the synagogues that Jesus is the Son of God"* (Acts 9:20).

I did the same thing. I started to preach Christ to everyone on the street or anywhere that I went. I told them it's important to know the truth about the Lord Jesus and accept his work for our sake, because he is the Way, Truth and the Life, and nobody can come to the Holy Father without Jesus. I had a deep love for my precious Jesus, and I felt sad for anyone who was far away from Christ.

On one very cold Netherlands' night, I was in a deep sleep after a long hard day, when I had a dream that I will never forget. I saw one of my lovely Christian sisters, whose name is Luna, approach me and give me a gift. I asked her, "What's this?" She said, "This is chapter 45 of Isaiah. Take it. It's yours!" When I woke up, I ran to my Holy Bible and before washing my face or brushing my teeth, I read Isaiah 45:

> *This is what the LORD says to his anointed, to Cyrus, whose right hand I take hold of to subdue nations before him and to strip kings of their armor, to open doors before him so that gates will not be shut: I will go before you and will level the mountains; I will break down gates of bronze and cut through bars of iron. I will give you hidden treasures, riches stored in secret places, so that you may know that I am the LORD, the God of Israel, who summons you by name. For the sake of Jacob my servant, of Israel my chosen, I summon you by name, and bestow on you a title of honor, though you do not*

*acknowledge me. I am the L*ORD*, and there is no other;*
apart from me there is no God. I will strengthen you,
though you have not acknowledged me, so that from the
rising of the sun to the place of its setting people may
*know there is none besides me. I am the L*ORD*, and there*
is no other.

I felt like I could fly to the sky out of happiness. The passage was long but the first three verses were for me! The Lord was telling me he would walk in front of me, would level mountains, would break down the gates and cut the bars of iron and would give me hidden treasures. How amazing! Was it possible that God would do all of this for me? I couldn't believe it. I was beaming with joy over this beautiful gift.

You can imagine that I read this passage many times and my heart couldn't believe the wonderful promises that the Lord had given me in a dream. After I washed up, I knelt to pray and thank the Lord Jesus. I got up and called Luna, who gave me this chapter in the dream, and thanked her for the beautiful gift. She was amazed and didn't understand what I meant, so I told her about the dream. She said to me, "Sister, this dream is a blessing to me and the verses there are for me, not for you." So I said to her, "No, dear, you are the one who gave these verses to me and the Lord used you to give me this beautiful piece of news."

We discussed this further and agreed that these Bible verses were for both of us, indeed for everyone who needs these wonderful divine promises. We can rejoice that our hard days do end, and that the Lord will open closed doors.

Letter from immigration

A day came when I received another letter from immigration, firmly confirming that I had to leave the country in less than a month. The letter gave me a date for an appointment with one of the officials in the government.

Whenever I received such letters, I was afraid and troubled because I didn't want to go back to Iraq, especially after accepting the Lord Jesus in my life. My return to Iraq would mean certain death! But this time, I wasn't troubled because of the divine promise to me. The Lord Jesus had promised that he would level mountains and break the bronze and steel doors before me.

Yet, I had short vision, and I didn't know how he would do this for me or how his promises would be fulfilled. Of course Matthias, who took me to the immigration department, knew my fears and was trying to calm me down on the road. He said not to worry because he and the church would stand by me until the end, and would never leave me.

The appointment was conducted by a serious Dutch woman with a threatening voice. She asked me what I understood from the letter, and I replied with unusual calmness. My composure surprised her. She was trying to intimidate me with threats that I had to leave the country, and her voice was getting loud. But I raised my eyes and looked above her head where Jesus appeared to me. He told me not to be afraid because he was with me, and reassured me that her speech didn't have any authority over my future, because my future was in his hand.

Matthias was watching my calm demeanor and was quite surprised and happy for the peace that lived in my heart, and for my faith in God's promises that he'd seen me repeat and write and hang on the apartment doors and on the walls. These are the promises that I held on to, and that helped me be strong and calm in the face of this impossible situation:

> *The LORD himself goes before you and will be with you; he will never leave you nor forsake you. Do not be afraid; do not be discouraged* (Deuteronomy 31:8).

> *No one will be able to stand against you all the days of your life. As I was with Moses, so I will be with you; I will never leave you nor forsake you* (Joshua 1:5).

> *Have I not commanded you? Be strong and courageous. Do not be afraid; do not be discouraged, for the LORD your God will be with you wherever you go* (Joshua 1:9).

> *The LORD is a refuge for the oppressed, a stronghold in times of trouble, Those who know your name trust in you, for you, LORD, have never forsaken those who seek you* (Psalm 9: 9 – 10).

> *But those who hope in the LORD will renew their strength. They will soar on wings like eagles; they will run and not grow weary, they will walk and not be faint* (Isaiah 40:31).

> *So do not fear, for I am with you; do not be dismayed, for I am your God. I will strengthen you and help you I will uphold you with my righteous right hand"* (Isaiah 41:10).

> *For I am the LORD your God who takes hold of your right hand and says to you, "Do not fear; I will help you"* (Isaiah 41:13).

Indeed, I continued to stay in The Netherlands for months after that with no one coming after me.

God begins to work in his unexpected ways

During this time, we heard that there was an Arab Minister, Pastor Malki, coming from The United States to hold meetings in The Netherlands. This was very exciting news for our church, and I was especially eager to help. My friend Sylvana and I were given the responsibility for organizing the meetings that were to be held in Rotterdam and The Zending (The Dutch church that we were attending.)

We began to pray daily and to call people to tell them about the conference. We faced several challenges in getting people to commit. First of all, the event was being held in a village in the forest with no way to get to by metro or train. There was an occasional bus, but the main transportation method would have to be by car. Our problem was that most of the Arabs in The Netherlands didn't own cars.

Secondly, the conference was scheduled to be held in April, right in the middle of the cold season when we often had snow. It was also to be held during the week when people had school and work. We started to pray for the Lord to open all these closed doors and send a real revival.

I was calling people every day and spending at least half an hour with each of them over the phone, talking about the conference, explaining how to get to the church, trying to match them up with other people living in their same area so they can ride together, and trying to answer whatever questions they had. Often, after a very long phone conversation, they would apologize and say they couldn't make it due to the distance or weather.

When the time came, everything was arranged; the hall and music and program. The night before the meeting we (The Branches of the Vine Group) gathered together at a specific time to pray, each in his house and on the telephone. We prayed with passion for this meeting, though we didn't know what to expect. We prayed that even if no one came, the most important thing would be for the Lord Jesus to be present, for if two or three were gathered, the Lord Jesus would be in their midst. We were content just to feel the presence of Christ.

On the day of the conference, I went very early to set up everything and to prepare the music. I was expecting to see very few people there. But the Lord blessed us with a wonderful meeting and many people came despite the weather, the strong storms and the cold. People had arranged their own carpools and helped each other get there.

Many came forward seeking healing and prayer for their difficult life situations. They were coming in faith to receive salvation and healing. At the end of the meeting, I was helping organize everything before I left. I went to Pastor Malki and asked him to pray for me. He asked me what my request was and I told him I needed the Lord to facilitate my immigration. I explained that I had been a Muslim and I had left Islam because of the love of Jesus Christ, but that people didn't believe me. I told him how much pain this had caused me, so he raised his hand to my head and prayed for me, then left the hall.

The meeting was finished and we were all very happy for the blessings that had been poured out by the Lord on everyone who attended. I never knew that day that what happened at this little conference would change my life.

2

Going to America

An unexpected invitation

The days were passing quickly and I was praying intensely for the Lord to do something about my immigration, but nothing happened. I attended all the church's weekly meetings, bible studies, and revivals. Whenever there was an opportunity to learn about the Lord, I would jump at the chance to listen to the Word of God and quench my continual thirst. This continued on for several months after I had received the notice to leave the country, but no doors were opening for me to leave.

One day, I had a conversation with a brother in the church whose name was Bashar. He was doubting that I had come to the Lord Jesus with all of my heart. He said, "If you love the Lord Jesus,

207

why don't you ask your God to give you residency? Why is your God not kind toward you? This is such a simple thing for him, so why is he letting you continue suffering?"

I didn't let this discourage me, but I assured him that God would intervene on my behalf. And just after this conversation, something amazing happened!

I had a surprising phone call from the American minister who had spoken at our little conference in the village. He asked, "Would you like to come to America?" I could not believe his question! I didn't know what to say, I was in so much shock. I was both ready to burst with happiness and ready to think it was all a joke. But in my heart I heard a voice from heaven speaking to me through Psalms 91: 14 – 16:

> *"Because he loves me," says the Lord, "I will rescue him; I will protect him, for he acknowledges my name. He will call on me, and I will answer him: I will be with him in trouble, I will deliver him and honor him, With Long life I will satisfy him and show him my salvation."*

The voice of the Lord was quite clear to me, and tears started to flow from my eyes. The minister said, "Answer me quickly, because I need to know your answer now." I told him that I would certainly love to go to America. He said OK and immediately hung up.

After the phone call, I knelt in front of my living room window and looked up to the sky and cried: "I thank you Lord! Is it true that I will go to America? Was that call just a dream or was it your voice, Lord, telling me that you're going to save me from the way I'm living now?"

On one hand, I told myself to be happy, but on the other hand, I thought I should forget about the phone call and not hold on to illusions that would never happen and end up even more disappointed. My situation in The Netherlands was critical. My case had been rejected by the government, I didn't have an Iraqi passport, and my Dutch residency had expired. How was I to continue living in such a situation?

Yet I had a great peace because Jesus was walking with me and listening to my prayers. So I decided to forget about that phone call and live as if it hadn't happened at all. Each day, I woke up early to pray and read the Holy Bible, then I went to language school and work. In the evening I would come back home to do my school homework, and this went on for about three to four weeks.

A dream comes true

One afternoon, I found a letter in my mail box, formally inviting me to come and work in the United States of America! I can't describe to you my happiness at that moment. I immediately called Pastor Malki in America to tell him that I had received his invitation. I asked why he had called me and invited me to come to America. He said, "It was the voice of the Lord! The Lord told me clearly to send you this offer, and I obeyed his voice." He continued, "Now go to the American Embassy with your passport..." but I interrupted, "I don't have a passport! I lost it and they won't issue me a new one."

He said, "You must get a passport, because without it you will not be able to come to America. Go to the Iraqi Embassy and have them issue a new Iraqi Passport for you." I told him that I couldn't do that because I didn't have a Dutch residency. He said, "Take the letter that I just sent to you and any evidence you have to prove your ID."

My happiness dissipated when I started to face the initial difficulty of not having an Iraqi Passport, but I took the invitation letter and placed it under the Lord Jesus' feet in the place that I prayed daily. I gave him the letter and started to thank him, "Lord, is this offer from you or not? O Lord, how I would love to go to the land of dreams, America, but now that it might happen, I'm afraid because I don't know anybody in America, and I want to make sure that this is your will."

I called Matthias about this matter and asked him to pray for me because I was starting to feel a lot of fear. I also asked him to take me to the American Embassy to ask about the visa. He called the Embassy to set an appointment for two days later.

We drove to Amsterdam to find the Embassy. The traffic was unusually bad and we were having trouble finding the address. The appointment was for 10am and we were still lost at 15 minutes before 10:00. I started to pray earnestly and we found the building but had to park quite far off. We started to run but Matthias was faster than me and I was far behind. He would keep looking back and calling me to hurry. The cold and fog and heavy clothes made it hard to run. My heart was beating very quickly and I felt I was going to faint. I was completely out of breath.

Poor Matthias' face was red with fatigue and he continued screaming for me to hurry but I felt like I was dying and had to

210

slow down or faint. When we reached the door, it was past 10am. The guard at the door asked us why we were there. I could hardly talk but muttered that I was there for a visa to America. He said he would open the door but I had to go in alone. I was distressed because I wanted Matthias to enter with me, because he understood things much better than I did and spoke the languages better than me. My Dutch and English were still poor. But Matthias encouraged me, "It's OK, go on your own and the Lord Jesus will be with you and help you. He's a better help than me, and I will pray as I drive home." What a beautiful man of God Matthias was, and I discovered that the Lord had put him in my life time after time to teach me his way.

Who is this uncircumcised American?

I was so grateful to the Lord Jesus that I had entered the Embassy. After checking me over twice, they had me wait for an hour in an outdoor waiting area. I was shaking with cold even though I was wearing heavy clothes. I became as stiff as a piece of wood. Finally the door opened and a man in uniform asked me what I wanted. I told him I wanted a visa to the United States. He immediately asked for my passport. When I said I didn't have one, he was surprised and asked what kind of papers I did have. I said I had the application and an invitation letter from a minister in America offering me a job. I also had a Dutch ID proving my address in The Netherlands, but it had expired over a year ago and was not renewed due to the rejection I got from the Dutch government.

211

When the officer heard that I had no other documents, he laughed out loud as if he was watching a comedy show. He said sarcastically, "You want to get a visa with these documents? Get out!" But he took the documents and shut the door in my face. He thought he was talking to a crazy woman.

I felt so insulted, and remembered young David, weak and thin, with his brothers mocking him, challenging the giant Goliath. I raised my eyes to heaven and cried to my Lord Jesus, and talked to him freely as usual because he was not only my Lord, but also my friend. I told him in a distressed voice:

> How can you allow this man to insult me? O Lord, who is this uncircumcised American to insult your daughter? He doesn't know who he is talking to! He shut the door in my face and left me out in the cold, but you, Lord will let me win and will let me not only into the Embassy to get the visa, but also into America, because you can, O Jesus, yes, you are able.

I kept talking to the Lord Jesus as a friend and forgot myself, until I heard footsteps behind me. I lowered my voice when I saw more people coming to stand in line. I told the Lord I would continue talking to him later because there were people behind me now.

After a while the door opened and the same officer told me to come in. I was so happy, thinking that my prayers had been answered. They checked me again and gave me my papers and sent me to window number 1.

212

Challenges and Miracles

The first challenge: Documents are needed

At the window, an American lady asked me if I wanted a visa to go to America. I said, yes. She said that I first had to get an Iraqi Passport, and would have to go to Germany, Belgium or France to get one. She also said I had to produce certain documents the next time I came. She gave me a list and said, when I have the passport and the documents, I should come again for another appointment. She then closed the window on me, thinking she would never see me again. I looked at the list she gave me. There were about ten documents that I had to bring in the next time!

I left the Embassy full of despair, and told the Lord Jesus that I thought this offer to go to America was not from him, because the doors seemed to be firmly closed. I took the train back to Rotterdam, and went immediately to inform Matthias what had happened. He asked me, wondering, why the employee had asked me to bring the passport from another country and not from The Netherlands? But I hadn't even thought to ask why. It wasn't until several years later that I found out the answer.

Matthias told me, "Don't be afraid. I'll take you to Belgium to get an Iraqi Passport in the Iraqi Embassy there, since it's the nearest country to The Netherlands. But we need to really pray and start working on getting all those other required documents."

I went quickly to my house and called the American minister asking him to send some of the requested documents. I called the

Iraqi Embassy in Belgium and confirmed an appointment for Tuesday to get a passport. Then I got to work on getting the documents that proved my identity.

A miracle: God's Word protects my documents

Early on Tuesday morning, Matthias picked me up at the Metro station to take me to Belgium. I was quite afraid because I was taking a big risk leaving the Dutch boarders without any passport or official papers. This was considered an international violation, and if I was checked by the police, they might take me to jail. But because the European boarders were all quite open to each other, I prayed the Lord would let us pass into Belgium unchecked. And he did!

We finally entered Belgium after a three hour drive. We were praying throughout the drive, I with my eyes closed, and Matthias while concentrating on driving. I felt exhausted by the intensity of prayer and crying to God, and my mouth dried up. So I reached into my bag to get a bottle of water I had quickly thrown in with my original documents that were required by the Embassy. To my shock, the bottle was empty. It had spilled into my bag. I screamed loudly and Matthias almost crashed the car.

I was so afraid that the water had destroyed the documents, but when I investigated closely, I was amazed to see my small Bible, which I had put beside the documents, tripled in volume! The Word of God had drunk all the water and protected all of my official documents. There was not a drop of water on them. This was the greatest miracle of that day and we began praising God for his goodness and protection and presence with us in the car.

At the embassy in Belgium I was told that my appointment was for Tuesday of the following week! I begged and explained that I had come a long distance from The Netherlands, but they would not see me. They wanted me to leave my documents with them, but I wouldn't. I was so embarrassed to go back and tell Matthias that he had driven me 3 hours each way for nothing. I was so sure he would scold me and stop helping me, but I knew that he had every right to be angry after what I had put him through with his already busy schedule.

That godly saint didn't get angry at all, but said, "Don't worry, all of this will work out for good." His response was so beautiful and I felt so bad and couldn't stop apologizing. I said, "It seems the trip to America is impossible. We can't even get through the first step. How will I be able to do this?" He said, "The Lord will manage everything." My dear friend and Pastor Matthias is truly a man of God who lives the Bible in his actions as well as his words. The fruits of the Holy Spirit are evident in his life: Love, peace, joy, patience, self-control, kindness, goodness and faith. The Lord gave me a great gift when he put this person in my life to help me.

Matthias apologized that his schedule the next week was totally booked and he would be at a conference in London. He promised to send somebody to help me. I was upset, of course, but I knew that what had happened was my own fault. So I kept praying all week and begging the Lord, "O Lord, please facilitate my going to the Embassy. O Lord I truly want Matthias to come with me because he's such an honest and loving and patient and smart person and when I'm with him I feel as secure as I do with my own father. But, Lord, let your will be done!"

The week passed quickly, and I was overjoyed when Matthias told me that he would be able to go with me if I took the train and met him in a city in the south, which would be on his way as he returned from his conference.

> *I lift up my eyes to the mountains. Where does my help come from? My help comes from the Lord, The creator of heaven and earth* (Psalm 121).

My beloved God, Jesus, had responded to my prayers.

I met Matthias in that city and we kept lifting up our praise until we reached the Embassy where everything went perfectly and the Lord's hand was with me and I took the Iraqi Passport! All our thanks and joy were in the Lord.

The second challenge: Back in the American Embassy

A few days after acquiring the Iraqi passport, I received a big envelope from the minister in the United States containing all the required documents for the American Embassy. I went by myself this time, in the power of the Lord, and with the required documents. They let me in quickly, and when the same officer who had ridiculed me the last time asked me the reason I was there, I said with confidence, "I'm applying for a visa and here is my passport and all the documents that you asked for."

I was checked again and left to wait my turn in a hall full of people. I had the Holy Bible with me, so I started to read in 1 Corinthians, and the Lord spoke to me through a beautiful verse which gave me peace, *"Because a great door for effective work has opened to me, and there are many who oppose me"* (1 Corinthians 16:9).

I waited a long time and they never called me. People who came after me went in, but my name was not called. Fear started to enter my heart, but I immediately remembered the verse that the Lord gave me and rebuked the devil in the name of Jesus. I knew the Lord Jesus would open the door for me to go to America. After everyone had been called in, I remained alone in the hall. I had been there over five hours. Finally they called my name and I went to the window.

The American woman spoke to me from behind the window, "Do you know why we kept you to the end? Because we want to talk to you honestly. Your case is not clear to us and we have a lot of questions and don't want to embarrass you in front of people. We have many doubts you need to clear up for us."

This troubled and worried me greatly. She continued, "We read the file and found that you are an Iraqi, and don't have residency in The Netherlands. We don't know why you are in The Netherlands and why you want to go to America? You are Iraqi and that means you should be in Iraq, and should apply for the visa from there."

I simply answered her that I had lived legally in The Netherlands but my residency had been rejected and I had the documents to prove this. I presented a paper from Matthias proving that he knew me very well and was ready to come to the Embassy and

217

talk to them. I also presented a paper from a lawyer proving that he was following up with my immigration case in The Netherlands. The consulate lady was listening to me carefully, and asked me what I was going to do in the United States and many more questions.

Eventually, she closed the glass window and pressed a button and within a minute a group of Embassy workers gathered around her, discussing something behind the closed window. I immediately started a conversation with the Lord Jesus as usual:

> O Lord, I ask you at this moment to come to this room behind the window where the consulate employees are gathered and take a look from your heaven at the computer. I ask you, beloved, to create a law for me and put it in front of their eyes on the computer now—some law that would be applicable to my situation. If your will is to let me go to America, O Lord, please touch the computer and change the entire screen for my benefit.

During my prayer, I saw the consulate lady point to the screen and say to the others, "I can see here a law..." I was so thrilled and said, "Indeed, O Lord, you have made my heart happy, and responded quickly, and kept your promise in Isaiah 65:24, 'Before they call I will answer; while they are still speaking I will hear.' My love Jesus, I love you, I Love you, I Love you more and more."

She opened the window and told me in a gentler tone, "You can have the visa to America, but we still need you to bring these additional documents from your American employer. If you bring them next time, you will get the visa." She gave me a list of about ten more papers to bring.

I left the Embassy depressed because I had been expecting to have the visa after what I thought was my joyful answer to prayer. I blamed the Lord saying, "Why, O Lord, do you deny me my happiness? I don't know if you want me to go to America or not, and if this is your will, why don't you facilitate this for me quickly."

I called Pastor Malki, and told him about the required papers I still needed, but this time he was upset and was ready to take back his offer. I told him we were now in the final stage, and maybe this time, I would get the visa.

The visa

The papers were quite delayed, and I thought that the minister had decided not to complete them. Finally, after many prayers and patient waiting, the documents arrived from America. I took them to the Embassy. Things were much easier this time because I knew the way and my heart was full of unusual joy and peace and confidence that I would hear good news that day. I didn't have to wait very long this time and the lady was actually surprised to see me with all the documents she had requested. She asked many questions and then told me to leave the passport with her. She said they would send it to me with a visa stamped on it for one year.

I couldn't believe my ears! I smiled broadly and wanted to hug this woman and kiss her because she had approved my visa. This was the first time I had felt secure for years. Within two weeks, I received my passport but with only a three month visa. I was confused! It should have been for one year, but still, I had a visa that would get me to the United States and I started to make serious preparations for my travel.

My last day of school

I continued to go to the Dutch language classes and didn't miss it once. I did my homework, even when I was working seriously on the travel documents because I wasn't sure if I would get the visa, and also, because I had a very good relationship with the other students. Most of my classmates were Muslims, and I was particularly fond of some of the Muslim women. I had always tried to invite them to the Christian conferences, but they didn't know anything about my Muslim background. I didn't want them to hate me. Muslims don't love other Muslims who leave Islam. I used to be just like them.

I loved to show my classmates the love of Christ that reigned in my heart, and I talked to them whenever suitable about the Lord Jesus and his great love and forgiveness. They always listened only and didn't ask questions. I even talked about Jesus with the Dutch teacher and she was happy when I prayed for her.

I had already bought the ticket to the United States and would be leaving the country within a month according to God's will. I wanted now to sow some seeds in this class before I left the country, and the Lord directed me to give every student the Christ Movie. I happened to have many DVD copies of the movie. It was the Christmas season of 2006 and the class was having a holiday party. I took 30 DVDs of the movie with me to the party in order to give them to the classmates and other students whom I might meet in the Cafeteria. I also took some delicious Arabic sweets and went to my class for the last time. Everyone shared some food from their country, a song or an activity. When my turn came, I sang this holy song that I loved very much.

> *O marvelous in his great love, O my Christ.*
> *You carried the sins on my behalf. I'm the sinner and you sacrificed for my soul.*
> *O Wonderful Counselor, Mighty God, Everlasting Father, Prince of Peace, O Jesus.*
> *O you are strong. You won over the grave and death when you rose*
> *And destroyed the enemies. You won.*
> *O My love, your love is sweet to my soul. It's my light.*
> *It's a healing and a medicine to my wounds, my happiness.*

One of the Arabic speaking students who was a Muslim was upset when he heard praise to the Lord Jesus. He began to utter some insults in a low voice, but I understood everything he was saying and was not discouraged. Afterwards, I explained the meaning of the song in the Dutch Language, and delivered the message of Christ, that he was the judge who will come in the last days, and I invited them to accept Christ.

After all of that, I distributed the DVDs to everybody and wished them a Merry Christmas, and said I would maybe see them on this earth or in heaven if they accepted the Lord Jesus as Savior of their life.

The third challenge: The unexpected happens

I was very busy with many last minute details before my travel date. I was energetic and full of joy, and the days passed quickly with me thanking the Lord every minute of every day.

Two weeks before my flight, I heard some news that shook me to the core. They said all current Iraqi passports in the world had been canceled and invalidated by the Iraqi government which would then issue new passports. When I heard the news, my heart sank into my knees and I fell to the ground crying loudly, "O Lord, what do you want from me? Please tell me!"

When I calmed down a little I decided to find out if this news was even true. So I immediately called the Iraqi Embassy in Belgium where I had gotten my passport. I was distressed to find out from them that the news was true. I told them I had an American visa on my existing passport. They told me that it wasn't a problem because the visa would be transferred to my new passport. I asked when this could be done and they said God knows how many months it would take.

I hung up quickly, screaming, MONTHS?! I felt so beaten, like a big door was closing in front of me. I prayed and cried, "O Lord, why do you let me go through that long journey and then close the door? I wish you hadn't sent the invitation from the beginning, and hadn't made me happy believing that I would be going to America."

After more prayer, I had the Idea to ask the Iraqi Embassy in The Netherlands about this news, and they confirmed it was true. After that, I checked with the Iraqi Embassy in Germany and I was surprised that they hadn't heard this news. As far as they were concerned, the old passports were still working. I was so happy to hear that, and I thought immediately that the Lord still wanted me to travel, but maybe through another country.

I remembered that my friend Remonda worked at the airport in Germany, so I called her, but she warned me not to travel through Germany. She encouraged me to go ahead as planned and not be afraid. She promised her church would pray for me, and she said that, if this is from God, nothing would stop me from getting to the U.S.

After intense prayer was raised for me at the church in Germany, I had peace in my heart for two weeks, but when the time to travel came near, the fears started to overwhelm me.

The next miracle: Saved from fire

It was the last night before my flight. Na'el and the rest of my dear Iraqi family came to pray with me and help me organize my final arrangements before taking me to the airport in the morning. We lit a candle and placed it in the middle of the table. I brought out my passport and we were laying hands on it and praying for God to bless my departure from The Netherlands without problems.

We were reading from the Psalms, praying and praising God when we heard the doorbell ring. The main building door was three flights down and I rushed down to open the door. It was my friend Huda and her husband Hasan, coming to say good bye to me. Everyone came down to chat with them and then we slowly made our way back upstairs. When I entered the room, I saw something that made me shake and scream with fear. The candle had burnt down and bent so that the flame was just a second from hitting my passport. I realized with fear that if I had waited one more minute, the passport would have been eaten up by fire and all my hopes would have gone up in smoke!

I quickly grabbed the passport and saved it, then fell to the ground, shaking and crying, "O Lord, why are these things happening to me? I am so tired of it all!" But my friends comforted me by telling me that the Lord had protected the passport because we prayed. Yes, prayer always saves me!

I slept fitfully that night because of stress and fear of what would happen the next morning at the airport. The fear was inside me although the Lord was also inside me. I was sure that the Lord was real and that he would protect me, but I couldn't help my feelings of anxiety at that difficult moment.

The day I left The Netherlands

I woke up early in the morning, as usual, and prayed and read my Bible. The 23rd psalm was my comfort and strength that morning:

> *The LORD is my shepherd, I lack nothing. He makes me lie down in green pastures, he leads me beside quiet waters, he refreshes my soul. He guides me along the right paths for his name's sake. Even though I walk through the darkest valley, I will fear no evil, for you are with me; your rod and your staff, they comfort me. You prepare a table before the presence of my enemies. You anoint my head with oil; my cup overflows. Surely your goodness*

> *and love will follow me all the days of my life, and I will*
> *dwell in the house of the LORD forever.*

My beloved family, Sylvana, Na'el, Matthias, and Alicia came in two cars to take me to the airport. We were singing and praying and I couldn't believe it was all happening. It was like a dream! Was I really leaving these amazing people that I loved so much and this beautiful country of love and magnificence, the country where I found the truth and met my beloved Jesus? I drank in the scenery as we drove—the clean and orderly streets, the people riding bicycles, the magnificent trees, the rushing river, the swarm of white birds flying happily over the car like a farewell party. I felt a strange love for this country, and an unusual nostalgia. I almost wanted to turn around and go back to my house and forget the whole idea of going to an unknown place.

My thoughts were interrupted by Matthias, "We're here!" When I saw the airplanes landing and the crowds at the airport gates, I was troubled again, remembering that my Iraqi passport was inactive.

We entered the outer gate, but just then, because of the cold weather and the anxiety I was experiencing, my heart started to race, the blood froze in my veins, and I couldn't walk. My friends screamed at me to keep going because the time was tight, but I couldn't. I begged them to pray and they did. Suddenly I found myself walking fast towards the first counter where they checked the passports and the baggage. They let me through without any trouble and we were all elated and singing Halleluiah.

We all went to have some coffee in the cafeteria, but Matthias urged us to go to the next check point. It seemed that he knew what was going to happen. I said a tearful goodbye to all my friends and got in line. When I reached the officer, he took a long time looking at my Iraqi passport, carefully checking the papers and concentrating on the pages. Doubts entered my heart when he started firing questions at me: "Where did you get this Passport? How did you enter The Netherlands? How did you get this visa?"

So many questions! I was about to faint from the fear that I was going to be arrested. He called someone and ordered me to go with the officer that came. He took me to a side room with about a dozen officers in front of me! They took my passport and started interrogating me like a criminal. Suddenly, the door opened and Matthias came in! I didn't know how he got in or how he even knew where I was, but I knew one thing—that the Lord Jesus had opened heaven and sent him to me to help me.

Matthias started to talk to them in fast Dutch sentences I couldn't keep up with. He was using a high level of tact to explain how well he knew me and he showed them papers from the lawyer to confirm that my presence in the country was legal. They started to search their computer records to see if there was anything illegal against me. They called the lawyer who confirmed everything we had told them.

Matthias and I sat in the corner to pray and ask the Lord Jesus for help. Outside, Sylvana, Na'el and Alicia were kneeling on the ground praying and begging for me. The time for my flight was approaching quickly and I was worried I would miss it. Suddenly, someone came and told me, "You, stand up! You can go to America, but we're putting your name on a black list and you may never enter The Netherlands again. You may leave this country now but you may never come back!"

I was so relieved and happy. I quickly said goodbye to Matthias and went running to the plane. Before entering the plane, there was another check point. Here again, they started questioning me when they saw my Iraqi passport. They asked me how I had gotten this far with it. I was so upset! I told them to call the management and find out from them. They called moments before the plane was ready to depart and at the last minute they told me my papers were complete and I could go onto the plane. I said to them, "Are you sure?" and then quickly followed the hostess to my seat on the plane.

I sat there in doubt, waiting for my name to be called and to be thrown out! But when nothing happened, I started to calm down. I called my friends on the mobile phone and told them that I was finally on the plane. Moments later, I was flying high up in the sky!

Above the clouds

It was a strange feeling flying above the land. I couldn't believe I was leaving this lovely country. I glued my head to the airplane window looking at the green land and flower gardens as they got smaller and smaller. There was something deep inside my heart that was being ripped up. For the second time I was being torn from my roots—the first time when I left Islam, and now the second time as I was leaving my second home.

When I was a Muslim, I was confident that I was living the right life and practicing the right religion. Then all my thoughts and beliefs were demolished and I lost all my family and friends. Now, I was leaving my beautiful new home where I had found the truth and known the love of better and truer family and friends. I felt a real pain in my chest, like the pain of having a tooth pulled by the roots.

So many difficult things had happened to me—from the government rejecting me, to my family disowning me, to insults and persecution, to tight finances... But all this trouble could never compare with knowing Christ Jesus, my Lord. I had gained the greatest treasure and the greatest love better than anything I had lost in my life, and greater than any trouble.

I felt right then how much I loved Jesus and how I had buried all my past life with him. I thought of the eight years that I had spent in The Netherlands and how surprised I was, when I first came, to see the elegance of the country, the orderliness of everything, the Metro, the trains. I thought of all the seasons with their unique colors and splendor. The Netherlands is truly a country created lovingly by the Creator. And the most important thing about this country to me, was that it gave me the Word of the Lord Jesus and introduced his great love to me.

As I thought about all this, I remembered that I was in a plane with a person sitting beside me. I didn't know whether or not he knew the Lord Jesus so I turned and started a conversation with him.

*   *   *

In The Netherlands,

I met you my great love, and you met me.

You planned and directed everything

To get me here and introduce me to yourself.

Right before my eyes, you closed the door,s

Filled my land with fog and destroyed everything around me.

Then you extended your hand and pulled me

To a beautiful country,

Shut the mouths around me,

Dealt righteously with me,

And opened my ears to hear your voice.

Here you gave me rest among strangers

And healed my every sickness.

But the most wonderful thing is that you extended your arms,

You looked at me with your eyes of love,

Pulled me into your heart,

Filled me with love,

And with your words you delighted my soul.

3

A Strange New World

When I arrived in California, the minister who hired me arranged for me to live with an American family. I was thanking the Lord so much, because this family knew the Lord Jesus, and we were all one in him. I started to go to church with them where the pastor and his wife, who happened to be Dutch, welcomed me warmly, especially when they knew that I had come from The Netherlands, and thought that I was Dutch. I saw the Lord Jesus' true love in Pastor Art and his wife Helma's hearts. They were very generous, welcoming, and humble in heart. I felt that I had known them forever. I started to go to church twice a week and got to know the lovely people there.

Very quickly after I came, I was faced with a clash of cultures and customs. I was surprised that when I reached out in love, I got negative reactions. One major example had to do with the family

I was living with. I was so grateful to them for letting me live in their home that I wanted to express my thanks by being helpful with the house work. I didn't want them to think I was taking advantage of their hospitality, especially when I saw both husband and wife work very long hours outside the house and then come home tired to cook and clean.

I started waking up early on Saturdays to clean the house. I also asked them if they liked Arabic food and started making my special kind of appetizers, and stuffed chicken with rice and nuts. I thought that I was pleasing them and helping them, especially the wife. But I was surprised to find out, after a while, that she was not happy, and was complaining to the minister I worked for. I was very hurt and I cried and stayed in my room from then until my boss found another place for me to live. Still I prayed for these people who were so kind as to host me in their home during my first weeks in America.

Help from Heaven

At that time, I had been in the United States for two months and only one month remained on my visa. I was scrambling to figure out what to do. I called a lawyer who told me not to worry, but I didn't understand how he could say that. I needed to know what to do. The situation was desperate.

I came home one night and prayed in tears, "O Lord, have mercy on me. In a few days, my month's residency will end and maybe with it my residency in this country -just like before. I need help. I am weak. Tell me what to do."

Two days later, a man came to the office where I was working in order to teach me how to work the computer system. He had worked in that office before me. As he was working on the computer, we talked about the immigration matter and he asked me to show him my passport. I asked why. He said, "You came to America with the same visa that I came with, and they gave me three *years* as residency when I was at the airport. Maybe they did the same for you and you didn't notice."

I told him that the passport was at home, and he asked me to bring it the next day and to look at the white card that was attached to it. I was so encouraged by this information and couldn't wait to get home to check my passport. It seemed to take forever to get home on the bus and I was crying to the Lord the whole time, "O Lord, have mercy on me! I beg you, God, to let my heart be happy and to show me your work. O Lord, just give me one year!"

I ran quickly from the bus stop and covered the distance in 10 minutes. When I got to my room, I went directly to get my passport and before opening it, I knelt on the ground again and was crying to the Lord, "Please, right now give me residency for one year and I'll be thankful, my God." I prayed loudly and earnestly from the bottom of my heart, and I was shaking as I opened the passport to look at the white card. I read it slowly and repeatedly. The big great surprise was that the residency on the passport was for three years! It was stamped on the passport at the airport, but they didn't tell me.

I could not believe my eyes! I read all the information on the white card again and again. I felt the arms of Jesus, my beloved, hugging me to his bosom, and the tears of gratitude just flowed out of my eyes. How great you are, O Lord. How wonderful you are, my beloved. I asked for one year, but you honored me with three years. I love you, O Jesus, and thank your my sweet Lord. Blessed be the Lord for listening to my cries. The Lord is my strength and my shield; my heart trusts in him, and I am helped. My heart leaps for joy and I will give thanks to him in song.

An abundance of grace

I was feeling relaxed and experiencing great joy now because I was living legally in the U.S. and had a visa for three years. But I started to think seriously about my future. Three years would pass quickly, and I had to seek permanent asylum.

I submitted my documents to the U. S. Immigration Department, and when the appointment time came, I gave them the whole truth. I told them everything that happened from the time I entered The Netherlands, to the time I met the Lord Jesus, to the time I entered the United States. After several months of waiting, I received a letter from the Immigration Department requesting documents from the Dutch Court. They wanted documents to prove that I had been rejected from residency there, papers from the city that I used to live in proving I lived there, and more documents that I thought were impossible to obtain.

When I read the letter, my heart sank within me. I called the lawyer immediately and he confirmed that it was a must to submit all the required documents. I told him that it was impossible, and that I planned to ignore this letter and not reply to them. He said that if I ignored an official U. S. government letter, it would look very bad for me and I would lose any hope of ever getting residency in the future. He urged me to try my best to get at least some of the documents. His answer was bitter in my mouth.

Where was I going to get papers that verified a Dutch Court decision to deny me residency? I hadn't brought any papers from there with me, so I called Pastor Matthias to see if he could try to help. He said he would try, but after a few days he called to tell me that the lawyer in The Netherlands could not help a person living in America. I was upset to hear this news and lost all hope of ever finding a permanent home. I was so afraid for my future and felt depressed.

I went home that day and tearfully prayed and begged the Lord to save my life:

> Oh Lord, I need your hand on me. This matter is so complicated, it's impossible. I'm in a tight spot. Please come now. It was you, O Lord, who brought me to this country, and you are responsible for me. Where can I go? What am I going to do? I'm in serious trouble, and I don't know what to do.

I felt I was drowning in a bottomless sea. As I prayed, I thought to get up and fetch all my paper work. So I brought out all my important papers, and started looking and crying and looking, hoping to miraculously find anything that would help my case. Suddenly something caught my eye. It was some Dutch papers. I dried my tears so I could read. I started to read slowly and to my utter astonishment—No, it can't be—a record of the final rejection of my case in The Netherlands!! Could that be possible?! How could such a thing happen?! The letter was right there in my bag!

My heart was beating with joy and I started to shout hallelujah, hallelujah, hallelujah. I kept checking the papers and found another document from Krimpen City confirming that I was living there. Hallelllllluuuuujaaaah! I shouted from the bottom of my heart and jumped to the telephone to tell the lawyer. He said those two papers were just what I needed. I couldn't believe what happened! It was a miracle beyond my imagination, and I knelt and cried happily:

> Blessed is the Lord because he listens to my voice and prayers.
> The Lord is my strength and my shield;
> My heart trusts in him, and I am helped.
> My heart leaps for joy and I will give thanks to him in song.
> The Lord is the strength of his people, a fortress of salvation for his anointed one. Save your people and bless your inheritance; be their shepherd and carry them forever.
> But let all who take refuge in you be glad;
> Let them ever sing for joy.
> Spread your protection over them that those who love your name may rejoice in you.
> For surely, O Lord, you bless the righteous;
> You surround them with your favor as with a shield.

The Lord Jesus himself had put those papers in my bag because he knew my need and cared for me like a shepherd cares for his sheep! I translated the documents into English and sent them to the Immigration Department. I was so joyful for what the Lord had done for me. I thanked him day and night because I knew I would get my American green card and have a permanent home at last. I trusted with all my heart that the American government would approve my papers and grant me the green card.

Waiting patiently for the Lord

As I waited to hear from immigration, I continued working for the minister who had hired me to come to America. I spoke daily on the phone with Arabs from all over the world, sharing the message of the Lord with them. I asked the Lord, every day, to allow me to lead people to salvation. He responded in amazing ways and I have been privileged in all these years to talk to many Arabs about the Lord, leading them to Christ, strengthening their faith, and praying for their needs.

Time passed without hearing anything regarding my immigration case from the government. The worries started to enter my heart again and people started to tell me that such a long delay was not normal and must mean that my case had been rejected. I was answering them that the opposite was true and, in the Lord Jesus' name, my case was not rejected. Inside, I was melting with fear and wondering why people didn't have mercy in their hearts, and instead of encouraging me and praying for me, they were making me afraid.

The wait was getting intolerable, so I decided to call the Immigration Department and ask them the reason for the delay. A message was sent to me saying that they were waiting to receive my papers. That was a big shock to me, and I realized that my papers had been lost somewhere. All of my joy was gone, but I went back and collected the copies of the papers and sent them again.

It was a few more months of waiting prayerfully and gratefully until I finally received a letter announcing the provisional approval of my residency. I praised God for his response to my need, and within two months, the Lord Jesus honored me with a Green Card during Christmas of 2013. It was his way of saying, "Merry Christmas!"

> *I waited patiently for the LORD; he turned to me and heard my cry. He lifted me out of the slimy pit, out of the mud and mire; he set my feet on a rock and gave me a firm place to stand. He put a new song in my mouth, a hymn of praise to our God. Many will see and fear the LORD and put their trust in him* (Psalm 40:1 – 3).

My life now- Sowing some seeds

I am now still living in the United States, still doing the same work I was hired to do all those years ago. Having a Green Card has allowed me to travel again. In fact, shortly after I came to the U.S., my youngest sister and her family moved to Germany. Some of my family had cut me off completely, but my little sister did not close her heart to me. I wanted very badly to see her but I had my fears of facing her husband who had been very upset when he found out I had changed my religion.

My sister, who is very tender hearted, spoke to him and convinced him to accept me and agree to welcome me into his house. My brother in law is a good man with noble character, high morals, meek, kind, contented and sincere. I made plans to go to Germany to visit them and the Lord was with me every step of the way.

All my brothers and sisters at church were afraid for me to travel because they knew what many Muslims did to people who left the Islamic religion. But, thanks be to God, my sister and her husband were not the type of Muslims who thought that way.

> **The Lord is my light and my salvation— whom shall I fear? The Lord is the stronghold of my life— of whom shall I be afraid?** (Psalm 27:1).

I took the Dutch airlines and was so happy to speak Dutch once again with the hostess. I still considered The Netherlands as my beloved country where I lived the loveliest days of my life and got to meet my beloved Jesus.

The plane stopped at the Amsterdam Airport for my connecting flight. When I stepped out onto the Dutch soil, I couldn't stop my tears. I remembered the harrowing time, only four years before, when I was in this very same airport, surrounded by police and forbidden to enter this country ever again.

It is my great God, the Lord Jesus Christ who rules my life and manages my destiny, not people or policies or governments. I will give thanks to him with every breath of my life, for all the good he has done for me.

An Invitation

Dear reader, I want to speak to you directly now—you my sister, brother, friend, uncle, cousin or maybe someone I don't know personally. If you are a Muslim, my words are especially meant for you. Now, you've come to know me through my story and have seen what God has done for me. Maybe some of the things in this book are things you've never heard before. Maybe some of the things in this book have shocked or upset you. Maybe you don't believe what you've read. But I tell you, before God, that what you've heard is the truth and now you must decide for yourself.

My prayer for you is that you would find the truth before it's too late. I wrote honestly about how the divine God broke through into my life. I tried as hard as I could to stay in Islam, and I defended it for decades. I wanted very badly to find the slightest excuse to remain a Muslim and keep the beautiful relationships I had with my beloved and dear family. But I found out without a shadow of a doubt that Islam could not protect me from the judgment of God for my sins or give me assurance of eternal life.

God in his mercy revealed himself to me because I asked him, and he will do the same for you. He will reveal himself to you if you seek him with your whole heart. It won't be the same way he dealt with me, but he will deal with you according to your heart, mind, and desire to know him. Yes, he will certainly make himself known to you if you earnestly seek him.

Ask God to show you his Holy face right now. You must not delay. You've read my words and I may be far away from you, but the Lord is very near to you, in the very room that you are sitting in. Kneel now on the ground and say from your heart:

> O My God, I was born a Muslim to Muslim parents, and lived all of my life in Islam. I pray and fast and follow your regulations and your prophet's teachings, but I don't know my eternal destiny, and I don't know what my fate will be. O Lord, I beg you, don't leave me on a path to destruction when I have spent my life trying to obey you.
>
> O Lord, you are the one who brought this book for me to read. Deal with me now like you dealt with the writer of this book and have mercy on me. I invite you Lord, the One True God, to come now into my life, live in my heart, and give light to my eyes so I can see you. Let me know you personally, and lead me to the way of the truth and the light which is your way, my God. You have put me on this earth for your glory. O Lord, I cry to you, broken. Please accept me as your child and deal with my weaknesses. Let me know your will and raise me out of my darkness into your wonderful light.

O Lord, I accept in faith the plan of salvation that was masterminded by you, my God, in the cross of Jesus Christ for the forgiveness of my sin. O my Lord, I'm anxious to get to know you personally, and have a sincere desire to follow you, even if you are not the God of Islam. You are my concern, not religion. My heart says to me to seek your face. Your face, O Lord, I will seek. Don't hide your face from me. Teach me your way, Lord; lead me in a straight path, because you are my salvation O God.

O Lord, I want to know which is your book? Is it the Quran? Is it the Holy Bible? Talk to me, O Lord, in the way you see fit. Let me know the truth about Muhammad. Show me if what I read in this book is true.

Thank you Lord, because you listen to my prayer and the cry of my heart. Thank you, Lord, because you will answer me and save me, along with my family and all my loved ones.

My friend, if you continue to pray in this way to God with a sincere heart and with humility, the day will come when you will receive the answer from God and you will know his way. God is tender and full of mercy. He will not leave his children for perdition, but he will teach them his ways and lead them to salvation.

My Muslim brother and sister, please accept the forgiveness of your sins and the guarantee of eternal life by putting your faith in Jesus Christ, the Redeemer.

And for those of you who have been born into a Christian family, or any other religion, or no religion at all, I hope you have seen the truth about Jesus with your own eyes. Accept the Lord Jesus

Christ as your personal Savior and Lord. Put your trust in Christ who was crucified on the cross and tasted a bitter death to save you from eternal damnation.

The word of God is very near to all of you. Believe in your heart and confess with your mouth that Jesus Christ is Lord, and you will be saved (Romans 10:9 – 10).

Salvation is precious, but God gives it to us freely. The price was paid by the Lord Jesus on the cross, and because of his blood, Christian and Muslim and all people can join their hands together with Christ and spend eternity together in joy and great peace.

Dedication

I dedicate this book to Zubaida Isaac Muhammad—my beloved, gracious, and devoted mother, who prays without ceasing, who sacrifices herself for others, who gives generously, who opens her heart and home to strangers. She lives by the strength of God and in fear of him. I am proud of her, not only because she is my mother, but because she is kind and respectful to all who know her.

My prayer for you, mother, is that God will give you length of days, and that he will touch your heart so you can know the Lord Jesus who died for you. May he give you salvation and security. I also pray that the Lord will bring his light into the hearts of my sisters and their children, my brother and his wife, all my uncles and aunts and their families, all my friends, and every Muslim person that I know and that I do not know. May you know and taste and see how great and righteous, kind, good, and strong the Lord Jesus is. May you know freedom from fear and all the chains of the devil.

I have spoken about my beloved Lord Jesus to many of my family, but they have not heard my words. They have accused me of blasphemy and sacrilege. But I pray that this book will reach them. I am not ashamed nor do I regret that I am walking this path, the path of the cross, but I boast in the One who died for me and gave me life, and saved me from my disgrace. I think of the words of the apostle Paul who said: **"I will boast in nothing but the cross of our Lord Jesus Christ."** He's not talking about the *wood* of the cross but the *sacrifice* of the One who is hanging on the cross.

I dedicate this poem to my mother:

Mother, you are more precious
than anything in my life.
I ask you to be happy for me
that Jesus has called me.
Come to me and call him Lord and Savior,
so he can keep you
and save you from sorrow and pain,
and death and the agony of the tomb,
just as he saved and protected me.
I used to always desire
never to lose your approval on my life,
but my Lord Jesus has to be first in my life
because he alone has rescued me.
He died on the cross for me and for you.
He wiped away all my trespasses
and sins and rebellion.
Pray and ask and persist in asking
So that you may gain eternal life

for he poured out his blood to give you the abundant life.
In Islam, my future was destruction,
but now I live a life full of joy and security.
I beg you, mother, don't lose your life
for the sake of Muhammad,
but wake up and be free from all your sorrows,
as I am free of mine.
And pray to the God of truth,
and don't be afraid of people
or Sheiks of Islam, no matter what they say.
For Islam is temporary and will not last forever.
Do not be stubborn. Listen to the voice of God.
I am afraid that every Muslim
will be destined for damnation,
and his life will be lost.
As for me, I have opened my heart to the truth,
and closed my ears to all that is false.
For Islam puts its faith in prayer
and covering and reading the Quran.
It's all just repetition and ritual without understanding.
I hoped that the Quran was the true way,
but now I know the Lord Jesus Christ
who rescued me from death and gave me honor.

Special Thanks

This book would not have been possible without the Lord's provision of faithful, godly people who love him and his Word. They have supported me and helped me to complete this humble testimony. I thank all my friends who stood by me through prayer, advice, and encouragement, led by the Spirit of God to produce something meaningful for the generations to come. I thank those who helped translate this book into English for me.

And I thank those who helped me financially and emotionally and spiritually even though they had many heartaches and difficulties of their own. Yet because the Lord has filled their hearts with his precious love, they continued to help and support me in bringing this work to light.

Words of Sorrow for our Martyred Brethren

Oh Lord, You said:

The world will rejoice but you will weep and lament.

And You also said:

You will be sorrowful, but your sorrow will turn to joy.

Oh my beloved perpetrators, when will you know

The Lord Jesus allows suffering so that you may repent and return to Him?

His kindness towards you ought to lead you to weep in repentance

And to be filled with sadness for all the innocents, and to see

That by your actions, you are walking the path to damnation.

You are digging your own graves and the graves of your own children

And you are making a pact with the devil.

Satan is your enemy. He is leading you to death.

Don't you understand?

Oh, dear innocent souls who have died in Christ, may you be blessed

Because you are now rejoicing with Him.

You have been lifted up

Like angels and returned in joy to your Lord.

We weep for you, but we know that, in Christ, you are victorious.

References

- Al-Rawd, by Suhaily
- Al-Seerah Al-Halabiya (Aleppo Biography), by Ibn Hisham
- Al-Seyar Wal-Maghazi, by Ibn Ishak
- Al-Tabaqat Al-Kubra', by Ibn Saad
- Authentic Quran; Commentary Quran, Literal Translation (Bilingual), by Little Jack
- Biography of the Prophet, by Ibn Hisham
- History of Tabari, by Al-Tabari
- Holy Bible, New International Version. International Bible Society.
- Holy Bible, New Living Translation. Tyndale House Publishers Inc.
- Islam and the Statue of Nebuchadnessar, by Al-Sheikh Muhammad Kamel
- Life Application Bible. Tyndale House Publishers Inc.
- Muhammad, Life Of, by Dr. Haykal
- Nisaa Al-Nabi (The Prophet's Women) by Bint Al-Shate'e
- Quranic Phenomenon, by Malid Bin-Nabi
- Sahih Al-Bukhari, by Muhammad Al-Bukhari (Islamic commentator)
- Sahih Muslim, by Muslim Ibn Al-Hajjaj (Islamic commentator)
- Sunan Al-Kubra' (Sunan Al-Bayhaqi), by Al-Bayhaqi
- The Glorious Quran-A Simplified Translation for Young People
- The Noble Quran- English Translation
- The Prophet's Wives, by Aisha Abd Al-Rahman
- This is Muhammad, by Musa Abd Al-Wahid
- Unmasking Muhamad's Life, by Joseph Shafi